KOI APPRECIATION

'Even the journey of a thousand ri begins with the first step.' (*Musashi*)

Koi
Appreciation

the first step

Kate McGill

The Crowood Press

First published in 2001 by
The Crowood Press Ltd
Ramsbury, Marlborough
Wiltshire SN8 2HR

www.crowood.com

This impression 2007

British Library Cataloguing-in-Publication Data
A catalogue record for this book is available from the
British Library.

ISBN 978 1 86126 468 8

Acknowledgements
A book of this nature could never be achieved without
input from many different sources. It would be
impossible to list the huge number of people who have
influenced my thinking about koi, and my knowledge of
koi appreciation over the years. Everyone I have talked to
has contributed something, spanning a vast range of
ideas from simple love of these wonderful creatures that
share our planet, to key issues concerning appreciation
and judging.

I would therefore like to express my thanks to
everyone, with particular mention going to fellow United
Kingdom, American and Japanese koi judges, past and
present, members of the British Koi Keepers Society,
Southern and North of England ZNA Chapters, and other
independent koi clubs in the UK. Further afield,
members of the Southern California ZNA Chapter, the
Mid-Atlantic and San Diego Koi Clubs, the Associated
Koi Clubs of America and the Dutch Koi Society.

Finally, special mention must be made of two people
who have made very important contributions to this
book: first, Joel Burkard of Pan Intercorp in America has
spent much time corresponding with me, assisting with
the verification of Japanese translations; and second,
without the other half of the McGill team, Andrew, and
his superb photographs of koi, my career as a koi author
and speaker would have been short indeed!

Designed, edited and typeset by Focus Publishing,
Sevenoaks, Kent

Printed and bound in Singapore by Craft Print
International Ltd

Contents

Preface

This is a book for all koi lovers, but particularly for those hobbyists who wish to progress beyond simple enjoyment of their koi. How do I classify a koi correctly? Why has this koi won its class? What constitutes a really superb koi? During my years spent gleaning knowledge about koi appreciation from every possible source, I have come to imagine how very pleasant it would be to have a good stock of basic, up-to-date information to investigate at least some of the answers to questions about koi, in one place! Taking this thought a stage further, I thought, could I write such a reference? I have at last made the attempt, and here it is: *Koi Appreciation: The First Step*, an introduction to what is essentially an art form, the joy of looking at koi and appreciating with wonder the intricate meld of colour and form that gives every koi its individuality, dignity and charm. The book is structured to provide a framework for everyone to build on, including basic information about classification and appreciation of each variety, as well as an overview of more general appreciation points.

It must be realized, however, that this book is not, and was never intended to be, a 'complete manual to koi appreciation'. The koi in this book are examined as finished koi, as seen from the eyes of a judge 'on the day'. The enormous field covering koi development and their potential for future excellence are areas that would fill a book in their own right, and are certainly beyond my scope. The aim here is simply to provide a frame of reference, to start everyone on the quest for the second step and beyond.

This book is dedicated to the memory of Seichi (Jimmy) Inouye, Koi Master of the Zen Nippon Airinkai (ZNA) Southern California Chapter, who believed that the demonstration of harmony and tranquillity by our koi constitutes a lesson we would all do well to remember. 'Koi is Love.'
(photo courtesy of Chris Bushman)

Introduction

Appreciation Defined

Asked to give my first talk about koi appreciation, many years ago, I first thought how easy it would be. I then thought about the word 'appreciation' and began to have doubts. I knew what I thought appreciation meant, namely to value something personally, with no regard to how the object of one's appreciation appeared to anyone else – but was that enough? If it was, then how was I going to give a talk about it? It would be the shortest and most boring talk on record, since my taste was hardly likely to be of much interest to anyone else. In desperation I consulted the dictionary, and this opened a new world I have been exploring ever since. Appreciation, in fact, means several things: 'estimating the value of'; 'understanding'; 'realization of good qualities'; 'to value highly'.

From this point I investigated further, consulting a famous word association book, *Roget's Thesaurus*. This proved to be even more illuminating, since it appears that the word appreciation may be used in many other contexts including 'choice'; 'selection'; 'critical appraisal'; 'discrimination'; 'differentiation'; 'arbitration'; 'adjudication'.

This means that, in the final analysis, a major aspect of koi appreciation involves judgement – bread and butter to a koi judge! Thus the path of my first, and many other subsequent talks, was assured.

1998 Shinkokai All Japan Grand Champion.

The enjoyment of watching koi.

Above: *Feeding time: having fun with your koi.*

Below: *Tame koi provide entertainment for the whole family.*

The Enjoyment of Koi

My initial reaction must not, however, be forgotten. Firstly, a very important area of appreciation involves the pure enjoyment of watching your koi, either individually or as a group, in an environment peculiarly their own. The grace with which koi swim is magic to watch – the way they use their finnage always reminds me of Japanese dancers displaying fans: the interaction of the wonderful array of colours with the patterns of light on water can be breathtakingly lovely, every turn bringing a new perspective.

The Personal Approach

We may also appreciate interaction with our koi: they often become very tame, and provide great joy in coming to the hand to be fed or even petted. I think everyone has a favourite: often it is the oldest, or the tamest, or perhaps one that has special associations. The point to really remember, however, is that appreciation of this nature involves a very personal approach. Excellence, beyond the health of koi and their environment, plays little or no part.

Evolution

The importance of this personal approach is readily manifest in yet another aspect of koi appreciation, after simple enjoyment of, and interaction with our koi: this is the way in which they have evolved. It is essentially personal choice that drives this hobby. From the very beginning, when early Japanese farmers decided to keep, rather than eat, their pretty, interestingly coloured mutant carp, the look of koi has been changing. By selecting genetically desirable, and in latter years saleable and show-winning characteristics, particular features have been stabilized and new varieties created.

Look at the progression of 'fashions' for Kohaku (a 'white-based' koi with red patterns). Many years ago the red (hi) was preferred above the lateral line only, whereas now, deep wrapping patterns are thought more elegant. Specific patterns such as the lightening stripe (inazuma) and separate head pattern (maruten) have had their day. Taisho Sanke (white koi with red and black patterns) have experienced similar changes to their hi patterns, with the addition of many variations in preference of size, number and position of black (sumi) markings.

Showa Sanshoku, a 'black-based' koi with red and white patterns, demonstrates perhaps the ultimate in pattern evolution. Modern (kindai) Showa are often mistaken initially for Taisho Sanke, the original predominance of black skin (up to approximately 60 per cent of the body surface) having been largely replaced by white, thus creating a much lighter, although no less imposing impression.

Varieties that were once quite rare have increased in popularity and numbers; these include the grey and brown Ochiba Shigure (autumn leaves on water) and the white-patterned, black doitsu (single rows of large scales along the dorsal and lateral lines only) Kumonryu.

Focus on the hi of Asagi-Shusui (blue, fully scaled and doitsu koi respectively, with red patterns particularly along the cheeks and lateral lines) is bringing in a whole new look for this variety. Hi is appearing on the forehead, as for Kohaku, and as an intricate pattern between the dorsal and lateral scale lines for Shusui.

Evolution of the essential character of our koi is therefore very much 'demand led', and so it seems fair to say that personal appreciation plays a large and ongoing part.

Quality

Finally, the aspect of koi appreciation that this book hopes to cover in more detail brings in words such as 'critical appraisal' and 'discrimination' to our koi vocabulary: the judgemental or comparative approach based on quality. The obvious questions then are: 'What is quality? How is it judged? On what criteria is quality based?'

A structured approach to koi appreciation is thus the next logical step, and this requires a certain amount of learning so that we may recognize the points that make one koi more acceptable than another in terms of quality. Many people are able to recognize a high quality koi without being taught, an innate skill, although they may not be able to explain why a particular koi is of a higher quality

Above: *A Marutan Kohaku, also demonstrating a deep wrapping body pattern.*

Above right: *Inazuma, or 'lightening stripe' Kohaku pattern.*

Above: *A Sanke with heavy 'old-fashioned' sumi.*

Above right: *A modern Sanke with much lighter sumi.*

Above: *A more traditionally styled Showa.*

Above right: *An example of a Kindai Showa.*

Right: *Spectacular improvements have occurred in some varieties – Goshiki.*

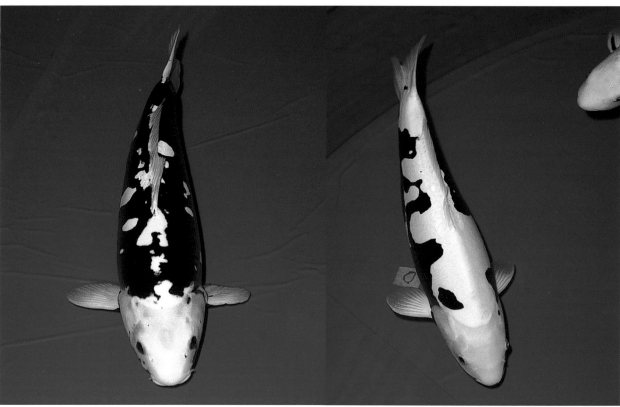

The highly variable Kumonryu, a currently very popular variety.

than another. It is important to realize, however, that this skill may be learned, and improved, by studying koi in the light of a group of essential appreciation points, and – perhaps even more important – that choice of a particular koi may then be justified.

A Structured Approach to Appreciating Koi

Points to be Considered are:

- The basic conformation of the koi, namely the shape of the head, body and finnage, including their relative proportions.
- The appearance and texture of the skin.
- The qualities of colour, pattern, pattern edges and pattern balance.
- The requirements of appearance specific to each variety, or variety characteristics.
- Deportment, or how the koi holds its position in the water and the way in which it swims. The health of the koi and the quality of its environment will significantly affect deportment.
- The impact each koi has on us, an area which very much sums up all appreciation points and which will be discussed at length in later chapters.

Conformation

The word 'conformation' means shape, form or structure. In using it, we are describing perhaps the most important feature of structured appreciation, the overall figure of the koi: the shape of the head, body and finnage, the interaction of the proportions of each, and how they work together. A strong, well proportioned figure gives the koi both power and grace, vital starting points to appreciation, although it is important to remember that we are not talking about a 'standard overall shape' for all koi. Considerable variation in conformation occurs, and in particular between young and fully mature koi. In young koi, impressiveness relies more upon pattern and finish than shape, since their smaller size and usually more slender figures cannot contribute to an imposing presence in the same way as for fully mature koi. It has been suggested that there is a 'crossover' point at about 40cm (16in), where overall shape and quality of the koi take over from pattern and finish in providing the greatest contribution to impact.

The Head

Generally speaking, the head of a koi tends to be broad and blunt-nosed. Mature koi, particularly

Pond visits: Appreciating the koi and gardens of other hobbyists is a wonderful way to learn more.

11

Above: *A well proportioned mature Kohaku. Note the smooth curve from the head and along the sides, and the attractive 'chubby' cheeks that many large koi develop.*

Above right: *A very nicely proportioned young Kohaku.*

Right: *Another popular variety, Ochiba Shigure 'Autumn leaves on water'.*

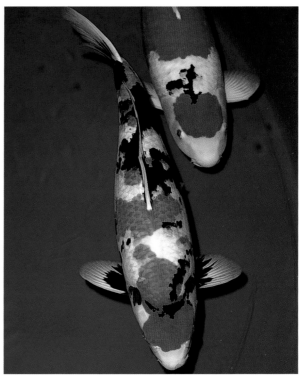

Sometimes quality is very easy to recognize.

This Showa is well proportioned, but quite differently to the Kohaku shown. Note the narrower head balanced by a much more slender overall figure.

Above: *This Hi Utsuri is not well proportioned: the head is too broad in relation to its length.*

Above right: *The head of this Sanke looks too small, and the bold sumi just behind the head amplifies this impression.*

Below: *A doistu Kohaku, showing a rather narrow head and shoulders.*

Above: *An Asagi where the widest part of the body is too far back.*

Below: *This Hi Utsuri is too thin – the widest part of the koi is across the gills.*

'Doris', a Sanke with the typical, fully developed Matsunosuke figure.

The leading edge to the pectoral fin should be straight, or gently curved along the entire length. Note the severe bend pictured on the pectorals of this modern Goshiki Sanke.

females, often develop 'chubby cheeks' on either side of the mouth, much loved by enthusiasts; these tend to make the head appear even broader and, in particular, more appealing – part of the 'character' koi may develop. Certain varieties of koi – for example, Chagoi (a single-coloured koi which appears in many different shades of brown) and Showa (a black koi with red and white patterns) – often have a narrower, more pointed head shape. This may have its origins in the introduction to the gene pool of the European carp in the nineteenth century. If extreme, this type of head shape constitutes a definite conformation problem. Another conformation defect that can occur is a head that is too short, nose to shoulders, or that falls too steeply in the vertical line from forehead to lips. The problems described have the effect of making the head look out of proportion to the body of the koi, and hence undesirable.

The Body

The body of a koi has been variously described as cigar-shaped or 'torpedo-shaped', which may be confusing, as each implies the same width of body at both the head and the tail end, with the widest part being in the middle. In fact the broadest part of the body of a koi should be in the area behind the gills, forward of the leading dorsal fin ray, giving the impression of strong, wide 'shoulders'. From this point a gentle taper occurs to, ideally, a thick, well muscled tail, or peduncle. On larger koi, this tapering may not begin until the leading ray of the dorsal fin is reached, giving a very strong impression to the koi. It is important, however, that the widest part of the body is not too far back from the gills, since this makes the koi just look fat, rather than impressive – a rugby ball appearance!

Ideally this basic shape presents a smooth line, leading the eye back from the head along the sides of the body in a pleasing manner. Much effort has been made in Japan to maximize the growth rate of koi while maintaining an excellent outline.

Bloodlines

Bloodlines play an important part in determining subtleties of conformational variation. For example, Matsunosuke koi are famous for their powerful and distinctive figure, although they lack the more pronounced curves demonstrated by other bloodlines such as Dainichi koi. There are also differences to be seen in the shape of the backs of koi, some bloodlines demonstrating a muscular shoulder hump, just behind the head – for example, the Manzo Kohaku line – whilst others have a much flatter vertical outline: Matsunosuke are again an example of this style. Many experienced hobbyists are able, at least in part, to recognize the bloodline of a koi by its basic shape.

The quality of this Kohaku's white gives a wonderfully delicate impression to the koi.

High quality white skin on a Sanke.

This Sanke's white skin demonstrates some yellowing.

High metallic skin quality is shown by the shine or lustre, seen here over the back of this doitsu Kujaku.

Signs of stress are usually manifest by reddening of skin and finnage.

Finnage

Finnage completes the picture. The length and shape of the fins makes or breaks the overall impression given by a particular koi. The pectorals are perhaps the most obvious fins, since these are usually held out to help the koi balance and manoeuvre in the water. The leading edge should demonstrate a smooth, straight, or gently curved outline; 'lumps and bumps' on the leading edge, or fin rays that are bent back acutely, do not look elegant. The trailing edge should be nicely rounded, delicate and well finished, with no fraying. The tail and other fins must be large enough to be in proportion with the head and body of the koi. Most important, all fins must be present, and the loss of any fin, or a large part of a fin, is a major conformation defect.

Finnage must also be 'clean' to give the best impression, meaning that the colour and texture of the fins should be even. Ill health may give the fins a bloodshot appearance; parasites and the virus carp pox may cause undesirable opacities or thickened areas to develop in the fins.

The Relative Importance of the Basic Figure

While it is possible to give an overall picture of what to look for in the basic figure or conformation of koi, it must be remembered that some variation due to breeding lines and stage of development is inevitable. Moreover, no single point of appreciation should be examined entirely in isolation, since it is always the interaction of all the elements that gives the final impact. However, it is true to say that if a koi has a really poor conformation – for example a bent spine, missing finnage or stunted body – there is little hope of a pleasing impression, even if all other elements are excellent. From this observation the vital importance of the good basic figure may be judged.

The Appearance and Texture of the Skin

'Skin quality' is a term that all koi keepers have undoubtedly heard at least a thousand times. Many will have scratched their heads and wondered what it meant, but been unable to gain a satisfactory answer. Others may have been afraid to ask at all, unwilling to appear ignorant. We hear many descriptions of skin quality: 'fair', 'lustrous', 'translucent', 'smooth', 'youthful', 'luminous', 'soft', to mention but a few. All apply to the concept, and yet do not really tell us what we are looking at.

It is perhaps easier to look at an analogy. Think of the difference between peoples' skin: there is a tremendous variation between young and old, in

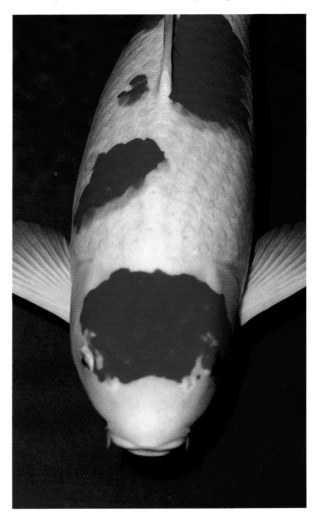

The hi on the head of this Kohaku lacks homogeneity.

particular, but also between men and women, and races – not just in colour, but also in texture. Everyone can admire a clear, fair complexion; for instance, we all know how soft and smooth a child's skin is, that wonderful (and fleeting) youthfulness! Think also how the skin of some individuals looks thin and delicate, whilst in others it has an opaque or grainy appearance. Then translate the differences to the skin of koi, and you will appreciate that the variations are just the same. A high skin quality on a koi will give the equivalent impression of delicacy, fairness and youthfulness; it will appear soft and smooth; scale edges will be hard to see; the colours will look bright, glossy, and almost liquid. One reason why koi breeders seek very early, rapid growth is that young koi, like children, will naturally have that extra bloom to the skin, so rare in later life.

Another interesting point worth mentioning here, is a possible explanation as to why male koi often lose their competitive edge as they age. It is not just lack of a comparatively impressive figure, but also that their skin may lose its delicacy more quickly than that of female koi, due simply to hormonal differences between the two sexes, a factor that has particular impact on the appearance of the skin in many species.

Using this approach of lateral thinking to skin quality, it is obvious just how important this appreciation point is, in structured terms, to the impact of any koi. Think again of a person with a lovely glowing skin. You tend to notice it very quickly. Going back to koi, even if other factors, such as balance of colour and pattern elements, are not what you would like, that basic high quality, bright, soft, lustrous skin would still shine through.

The Qualities of Colour and Pattern

More will be said about each of these points in the chapters relating to the varieties of koi, since often the requirements are quite specific. There are, however, some general areas common to all.

The Appearance of Colour

On a koi, colour will, as we have just explained, depend to at least some extent on the quality, age and sex of the individual. It will also largely depend on genetics, and which bloodlines have been involved in its breeding. For example, Manzo Kohaku are recognized for the strength of their hi, being a particularly rich and deep shade of red; whereas Sensuke Kohaku are much lighter, with a more orange-coloured and often thinner-textured hi. Lastly, the conditions in which koi are kept and their feeding regime, areas that are beyond the scope of this book, will affect the colours of koi.

When looking at any colour, be it white, red, black, yellow, brown, grey, green or blue, the most important feature is its homogeneity. To explain: the

A young Shiro Utsuri showing an exceptional combination of white skin and dense glossy black sumi.

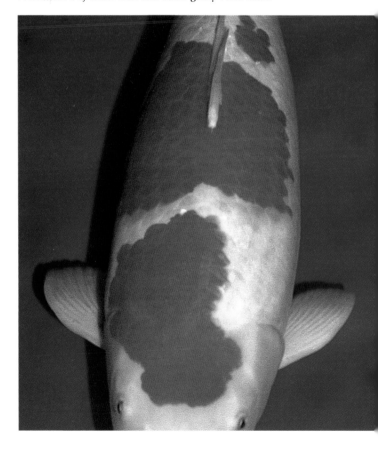

Close-up of second pattern element – sashi and kiwa of first element.

colour should look even within each pattern element and wherever it occurs, from head to tail and from one side of the koi to the other. An exception to note, is where colour appears on the head. It may acceptably look a little different in colour and texture to colour on the body of a fully scaled Koi, simply because there are no scales on the head. The impression is more elegant, however when the colour on head and body is near equal.

White skin should be as white as possible, with no yellowing. Male Shiro Bekko (white koi with black patterns) and Shiro Utsuri (black koi with white patterns) often have yellowish skin on the head that rarely improves to white, once it appears. The white skin of very young koi may have a pink (Kohaku, Sanke) or blue (Shiro Utsuri, Showa) tint, due to its transparency; but as the koi ages the skin becomes more opaque and the white colour should become clear. Again, depending on the variety of koi, the shade of white may appear slightly different due to the effect of colour interaction.

Thus, basically black koi with white patterns superimposed tend to have a 'cold', blue-white shade; this impression is exaggerated by the often deep blue tinted, scale-insertion point of sumi (black) underneath white at the leading edge of a sumi marking. White-skinned koi with red patterns usually have a 'warm', creamier tinted white.

It must also be noted that other base colours – for example, black, blue, brown, yellow, grey, green or red – must also be bright and strong. Ideally, no small spots or stains should mar the clear, clean impression of the colours.

Quality of Pattern

When a koi has more than one colour, quality of pattern, pattern edges and pattern balance may be added to the growing list of structured appreciation points. Pattern edges on fully scaled koi are interesting. They are looked at very differently, according to whether the edge is forward of the pattern element (nearer the head) or trailing (nearer the tail). At the leading edge of a pattern element, the insertion point of one scale underneath another, where two colours meet, often creates an area where the two colours look mixed and the edge in consequence looks blurred (sashi or sashikomi). The extent of this effect depends on the thickness and opacity of the overlying skin.

Above: *Although an eye-catching Tancho Showa, the sumi displays unevenness and poor kiwa.*

Right: *A Tancho Showa with dense, even sumi and superb kiwa.*

A Kohaku with shallow wrapping hi – komoyo.

Although the quality of the skin on this Showa is high, the pattern lacks balance. Sumi and a large motoguro dominate one side.

A Kohaku with deep wrapping hi – omoyo.

A godan (five-step Kohaku).

An unusual pattern gives unique appeal to this koi.

A doitsu Kujaku (Hikarimoyo) showing high lustre,
a very clean finish and good homogeneity of colour.

The BKKS (UK) 1994 Grand Champion, the 'Hook
Kohaku', demonstrates a memorable and well balanced
pattern.

This doitsu Hariwake Ogon demonstrates both uneven
colour and a pattern that is heavy at the head end
of the koi.

Goshiki with a clear vignette, or reticulation effect, over the hi.

The nose hi on this Sanke makes an otherwise almost bald head both acceptable and unusually attractive.

Goshiki with reticulation that lacks definition over both hi and white.

An Ogon, showing its interest in the photographer.

Introduction

A very alert Kohaku.

may follow scale borders (maruzome or uroko-kiwa), or it may cut across scales (kamisori-kiwa). The scalloped appearance of uroko-kiwa imparts a very delicate-looking finish to each pattern element and is generally thought to look refined. Kamisori-kiwa creates a more powerful, crisp finish, especially if the edge is on the diagonal across the koi.

Pattern Styles

These are very individual when it comes to appreciation. Some general points include the size of pattern elements, how far over the back they extend, and the relative proportions of colours involved – although there are no 'standards', just what is thought to create the best impression, a concept which changes over the years, as has already been mentioned. Any pattern, however, must fit the koi; therefore large markings on a mature koi are usually preferable to very many small markings, that give an untidy look. A pat-

Above: *The 1993 BKKS (UK) Grand Champion clearly demonstrates the power and elegance of pattern simplicity when coupled with high quality.*

Right: *The contrast which different varieties of koi provide together is a part of their magic.*

Sashi

The presence of sashi has often been said to demonstrate the depth and density of underlying colour, although it is generally agreed that for a pleasing impression, sashi should not involve more than one, or at the most two scales forward of any pattern element. The presence of sashi on some koi varieties has been deliberately selected for, genetically, in recent years: Shiro Bekko (a white koi with black markings) provides a useful example. Photographs of early Shiro Bekko, about fifteen to twenty years ago, show black (sumi) markings without sashi; the sumi looks to be floating on the white skin. Modern Shiro Bekko sumi tends to look much more solid and intrinsic to the Koi, with deep blue sashi on the leading edge of each sumi marking.

Doitsu Koi have few (kagamigoi) or no scales (kawagoi), and never demonstrate sashi. The leading edge of a pattern on a doitsu koi must be very clean and sharp.

Kiwa

The trailing edge of a pattern element (kiwa) on both fully scaled (wagoi) and doitsu koi should always look sharply cut. For wagoi, two styles occur: the edge

tern that wraps deeply around the koi is also thought to look more elegant and powerful, especially on large koi; a clear area of the base colour on the nose and just before the tail gives a neat finish. Since pattern edges are important appreciation points, stepped patterns (danmoyo) or streaming patterns (nagaremoyo) having deep inserts of base colour along their length are preferable.

Simplicity figures largely in pattern appreciation, as does the unusual. In this aspect, every koi is unique. No two ever have the same pattern, and this infinite variability holds particular fascination for koi lovers. The impressions of charm, dignity, character, elegance, even heroicness, may often be ascribed to how the different pattern elements work together.

The pattern on a koi is like a painting of a landscape, in that the eye should be led from element to element, head to tail. Many koi have one particular area where the pattern is eye-catching. However, if the rest of the koi holds no interest, the pattern may be said to be unbalanced. This commonly occurs when one colour is too dominant in one area, perhaps over the head. For example, menkaburi (a completely red head) on Kohaku, Sanke, Showa and Goshiki (a basic red and white koi with shades of blue and black as an overlaying scale reticulated effect, or vignette) creates a very heavy, front-ended image.

A pattern may also be confined to one side of the koi (katamoyo) or, when more than two colours are involved, the distribution can be uneven. Sanke and Showa often have their hi patterns concentrated on the front half of the koi, leaving the tail end plain black and white. Whenever a pattern is present it must involve the entire koi to give a balanced finish.

Deportment

In simple terms, deportment means the koi's orientation and appearance as it swims. A healthy koi, comfortable in its environment, looks alert and is interested in other koi and in anything it spots either above or in the water. It will be keen to feed, and will hold its finnage well spread out, and it will usually be on the move during daylight hours, unless temperatures are very cold. When at rest or when generally swimming, the head and tail are level with each other – unless, of course, the koi is engaged in some activity, for example, grazing the algae and small invertebrates to be found around the edges of any pond.

Deportment is particularly important when appreciating koi. The impression of proportion is affected if a koi does not display its finnage correctly. When a koi cannot orient properly, with head or tail up or down in relation to each other, or if it refuses to swim, no impression of grace or power is conferred. This is perhaps an area of appreciation not given sufficient attention in the past. We tend to take the movement of koi in the water rather for granted, yet the way in which they swim and use their finnage adds an extra, constantly changing dimension to how they impact on us, a vital element of the comparative approach.

In Conclusion

To continue further along the road towards understanding koi appreciation we must now look at characteristics specific to each variety, and to the many different koi within each group that share them. The aim is to create a picture, not of a perfect Kohaku, Sanke or Hikarimuji (for example), because perfect koi do not exist, but of those points which allow us to compare one koi with another, to judge their excellence and appreciate them positively. If an ideal exists in koi appreciation, it is to be able to perceive beauty first.

1 Kohaku

Kohaku at a Glance

A white koi with red (hi) patterns. Kohaku are named for specific pattern types i.e. Nidan (two step).

Ippon Hi	(straight hi, renzokumoyo, continuous from head to tail)
Nidan Kohaku	(two-step)
Sandan Kohaku	(three-step)
Yondan Kohaku	(four-step)
Godan Kohaku	(five-step)
Inazuma Kohaku	(lightening stripe)
Menkaburi Kohaku	(a completely red head)
Maruten Kohaku	(a separate head pattern)
Flowery Kohaku	(many small areas of hi; no recognizable step pattern)

Not Classified in Kohaku for Show Purposes

	Show Class
Gotenzakura (cherry pattern)	Kawarigoi
Kinzakura (golden cherries, i.e. gold-bordered hi)	Kawarigoi
Kanoko (dappled hi)	Kawarigoi
Kin-Gin-Rin Kohaku	Kin-Gin-Rin

Features

Hanatsuki	Head hi extends down the nose
Omoyo	Large wrapping hi patterns
Komoyo	Small wrapping hi patterns.
Danmoyo	Stepped hi pattern.
Kutchibeni	Hi on lips.
Motoaka	Hi on pectoral fin joints.

Kohaku

Doitsu	Either kagamigoi, having rows of large scales along the dorsal and lateral lines only; or kawagoi, having almost no scales at all.
Tobi hi	Very small hi spots.
Uwappi	Thin hi.
Bozu	No hi on the head.
Kirekomi	White inserts into the hi rising from the sides of the koi.
Nagaremoyo	Streaming hi pattern.
Hoaka	Hi over the gill plate.
Bongiri	The head hi does not come far enough forward towards the nose.
Beret hi	Asymmetrical head hi on one side only.
Asagi hi	Secondary, undesirable hi appearing as freckles below the lateral line.
Kokesuki	Colourless, or lighter-coloured scale-sized areas within a hi element.

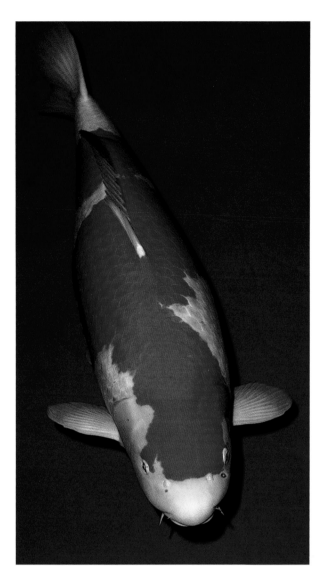

The 2000 All Japan ZNA Grand Champion provides an undeniably powerful impression.

Introduction

Kohaku is the Japanese name for a koi that has only red patterns on a white background. These fish appeared early in the nineteenth century, and the first 'Sarasa' – the name for a pattern of birds and flowers, or geometric figures on cloth – was documented at around 1830; this was the first time that red patterns had been seen on the back of the fish.

Evolution

Kohaku are said to have originated from the Asagi Magoi (blue/black netted wild carp). Two other lines of Magoi important to the origins of koi varieties are the Doro Magoi (mud carp) and the Tetsu Magoi (iron carp). These were all fully scaled (wagoi); the doitsu, or European carp, was introduced later and crossbred with several early varieties of koi. The very deep body and narrow head of the European line of carp is still seen today.

From Asagi Magoi appeared first the Konjo Asagi: an Asagi is a blue koi with a darker blue reticulated scale pattern and red, typically appearing around the koi below the lateral line. From the Konjo Asagi, (a very dark blue/purple Asagi), probably by selecting for lighter backgrounds and red patterns *above* the lateral line, the red and white Kohaku was fixed during the Meiji era, (1862 to 1912). Although earlier 'Kohaku types' existed, the famous Gosuke Sarasa, produced in 1889 by Kunizo Hiroi, appears to be widely accepted as the direct ancestor of modern Kohaku.

Intensive selective breeding since the 1890s has produced the Kohaku we see today. Important early bloodlines include first the Tomoin (1930s) and Yagozen (1940s), later followed by Buheita, Sankuro, Manzo and Sensuke Kohaku, names that are still well recognized, although it has been said that no pure-blooded koi now exist for some lines, for example, Tomoin.

A deceptively simple variety, Kohaku has been called 'the representative class of koi'; and the Japanese people say 'the road to the world of nishikigoi begins and ends with Kohaku'. This means, perhaps, that the beauty of Kohaku may be appreciated, in an artistic sense, at any level of the hobby. Understanding Kohaku is a profound study and, it is said, leads to understanding of other varieties that Koi keepers may prefer over the years. But a return to Kohaku when more experienced in appreciation is almost inevitable, because of the fascination that this infinitely variable, yet elegantly simple koi variety holds.

Basic Principles of Appreciation

Conformation

Appreciation of Kohaku, as for all koi, begins with the figure. A good, strong conformation – the overall shape, and the proportions of the head, body and finnage – provides that incredible impression of power, grace and elegance that is so essential as a starting point to the overall impact of the koi. In addition, defects of conformation – for example a very narrow, pointed head, or deformed, badly proportioned finnage – are particularly noticeable in a simply patterned koi, such as are many Kohaku.

Skin Quality

The second feature vital to general appreciation is the quality of the skin. The basic quality of the skin

The Shinkokai 1998 All Japan Grand Champion.

is often more immediately noticeable when there are fewer pattern components, and when a koi has a relatively large proportion of white skin, as do Kohaku. A koi's skin should appear smooth, soft and lustrous, a characteristic that gives large, mature koi a youthful appearance. Smaller, younger fish that have naturally better skin due purely to the age factor should look incredibly glossy and bright; scale edges should not be easily visible, regardless of the size of the koi. High quality skin gives the finnage of non-metallic varieties a delicate, translucent gloss.

The quality and colour of the white skin (shiroji) is particularly important for Kohaku. It should be pure

Left: *Lack of homogeneity of hi is a well recognized problem.*

Right: *A rather over-patterned Kohaku demonstrating heavy sashi.*

27

This doitsu Kohaku is rather too heavily patterned towards the tail for balance.

Clean white fins, providing a pleasing contrast with the hi on the body.

Above: *The delicacy of a maruzome kiwa.*

Above right: *A koi showing a nicely balanced finish, where hi and white are well proportioned.*

white with no yellowing, although a warm, creamy impression is expected due to its juxtaposition with the red pattern elements. If the basic skin quality is high, the white skin will appear soft, clear, uniform and luminous, with very delicate pectoral fins, even in large koi.

The highest quality red skin (hi) has an orange/red, rather than a purple base. It is more difficult to bring out well, but is usually stable when developed. Modern Kohaku, and certainly those of the major bloodlines, are more likely to demonstrate the orange/red hi. Tremendous effort has been made by koi breeders to improve the colour, texture, thickness and stability of hi, while maintaining other desirable features – an excellent figure, good white skin, vigorous growth – by crossbreeding various lines of Kohaku, for example Sensuke with Dainichi, Manzo or Izumiya.

Colour

Hi should look as though it has been painted thickly on to the koi. As the koi flexes, no flashes of white should appear at scale edges within any hi element. Ideally, scaling should not be obvious throughout the red areas, and the surface of these, when hi is fully developed, should look almost lacquered or 'polished'. Hi should also be homogeneous – that is,

A classic kutsubera (shoehorn) head pattern and inazuma body pattern.

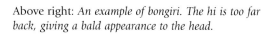

Above: *An example of beret hi.*

Above right: *An example of bongiri. The hi is too far back, giving a bald appearance to the head.*

A classic three-step (sandan) Kohaku, with a marutan head pattern.

A hanatsuki head pattern.

Kohaku

'Lady Di', 1996 BKKS (UK) Grand Champion.

An almost comical impression is created by the cheek and nose hi. Otherwise this koi has a rather plain sandan pattern.

even in colour and texture within pattern elements from head to tail – and it should have no blemishes. Small windows of white (madoaki), or faded, scale-sized patches of hi (kokesuki) within a large pattern element often point to impending deterioration or break-up of the hi.

It is important to remember that the main objective is to achieve a strong contrast between hi and white ground: the actual shade of hi is of less significance, and it is the relative depth of each colour and how they work together that creates the desired impact. There is an interaction between red and white for each individual koi, for example, a Kohaku with very bright, snow white skin would produce a higher impact, given a lighter, orange coloured hi, than would a Kohaku having a slightly darker, creamy coloured white ground. For the same degree of contrast and impact in the latter case, a much deeper, stronger coloured hi would be essential.

Sashi

The edges of hi, or other coloured markings, have particular significance when appreciating a patterned koi such as Kohaku. Remember, leading and trailing edges are looked at quite differently. On a fully scaled koi (wagoi) each scale fits partially under the one in front of it. Overlapping upper and middle layers of skin cover scales and carry the pigment cells. Where coloured skin is overlaid by white skin, at the leading edge of a pattern element, the coloured/white interface may look blurred: this type of edge is called sashi. It tends to be more common on younger, still developing koi where the white skin is more translucent, allowing the coloured middle skin, between and below adjacent scales, to be perceived.

Sashi only exists when pigment is present in the middle skin layer, generally thought to indicate long-term stability of colour. Opinions differ as to both the desirability and the appearance of sashi; for example, it has been suggested that if sashi is uneven, or extends beyond one scale-width forward of any pattern element, the (hi) pigment of the middle layer may be unsettled and its concentration undesirable. It is also thought that sashi appearing on the leading edges of the majority of pattern elements looks untidy.

The consensus of opinion however appears to be that, when showing koi, sashi is acceptable as long as it is limited to a few small areas and does not extend beyond one, or at most two scale-widths. Its presence certainly does not preclude a champion koi, as the 1998 All Japan Shinkokai winner affirms. Interestingly, the dominant Sensuke line of Kohaku is said to have hi pigment cells in both upper and middle skin layers – the most desirable distribution – yet these koi do not demonstrate sashi.

Kiwa

The trailing edges of pattern elements should always be sharp, and they look particularly elegant when the cut-off line follows each rounded scale edge (known as maruzome or uroko-kiwa, meaning 'a scalloped edge'). More commonly, the kiwa cuts directly across each scale forming a kamisori or razor border. The popularity of the Sensuke bloodline of Kohaku, which demonstrates this type of kiwa, has meant that Kohaku showing the maruzome edge (accredited to the Manzo bloodline) have become quite rare. Koi often demonstrate a blend of both styles of kiwa, a mixture known as konzai.

Doitsu Koi

It is sometimes thought that koi with no scales (kawagoi or leather carp), or with only single rows of large scales along the dorsal and lateral lines (doitsu or kagamigoi), cannot compete fairly against fully scaled koi. Pattern edges lack that third dimension of depth, which full scaling confers. In some contests, all doitsu koi are judged separately.

Pattern

Inexperienced koi hobbyists are often reported as concentrating all their attention on pattern, to the detriment of other vital appreciation points. In fact, the style of a Kohaku's pattern is not of prime importance, as long as the impression or balance is pleasing, and demonstrates relatively equal proportions of red and white. Although an attractive, highly individual pattern is very desirable, a plain pattern by no means excludes a high quality Kohaku from champion status.

Important pattern appreciation points include the size of hi markings. Larger markings, particularly on large koi, are more impressive. Balance is improved if the largest hi step (hiban) is over the shoulder area. Too much hi behind the dorsal fin (the ozutsu region) can give a heavy appearance, and many small spots of hi (tobi or niban hi) look untidy.

Ideally, a small area of white skin between the edge of the last hiban (odome) and the tail should be visible. This is especially pleasing if balanced by a white nose.

Hi patterns that cut diagonally, rather than straight across the body of the koi, are thought to provide a more elegant impression. Hi should never extend into the tail, and is preferred not to stain any other finnage. A clean white dorsal fin against a solid hi marking is very pleasing.

An exception to this general rule might be made by the presence of motoaka, or red pectoral fin joints; in conjunction with other pattern elements, these may look very attractive.

A kanoko Kohaku.

Any pattern should show relatively equal amounts of hi on both sides of the koi. A one-sided pattern (katamoyo) looks very unbalanced.

Secondary, or Asagi hi may appear as a freckled effect below the lateral line on Kohaku and other varieties of koi: this is an 'original' or throwback genetic feature, and is considered highly undesirable when expressed on a modern koi.

Categories of Kohaku Patterns

Several categories of Kohaku patterns may be defined:

Straight hi (ippon hi or renzokumoyo, a continuous pattern): Hi extends in an unbroken line from the head to the tail. This pattern looks very plain and excludes appreciation of the pattern edges along the length of the koi.

Lightning shaped hi (inazuma): This is an extension of ippon hi, in which the line describes a zigzag along the back: a streaming pattern (nagaremoyo). This pattern is very elegant, with insertions of white (kirekomi) skin allowing pattern edges to be appreciated more fully.

Stepped pattern (danmoyo): Blocks of hi appear along the back, separated by areas of white skin (doware). The pattern may be two step (nidan), three step (sandan), four step (yondan), or five step (godan). This pattern category allows full appreciation of all the desirable qualities for Kohaku.

Flowery hi: Hi markings do not form a recognizable step pattern. Pattern elements may be unusually shaped or small (komoyo), and very numerous.

It is important to remember that if a large, mature Kohaku is to look truly imposing, it requires hi markings in proportion to its size.

In the early years, hi markings that extended below the lateral line were disliked, as are those covering the gills (ho-aka). Latterly, however, opinion has changed, and it is now generally acknowledged that deep wrapping markings can confer a considerable impression of power to a large koi.

The Head Pattern

This area of pattern is important enough to warrant separate attention. Some hi is essential on the head of a Kohaku: a bald white head (bozu) looks unbalanced, as does the opposite extreme of a completely red head (menkaburi).

The classic Kohaku head hi describes a U-shape or shoehorn (kutsubera) between the eyes, reaching approximately halfway to the nose. A hi marking which extends to the nose but does not cover the eyes or cheeks is called hanatsuki.

If the head hi does not reach as far down as the line of the eyes (bongiri), a further hi on the nose and/or lips (kuchibeni) may add necessary balance, although there is much difference of opinion as to the merit or demerit of nose hi.

In recent years, uniquely shaped head hi patterns have become both acceptable and very desirable, often with asymmetric hi covering one cheek (beret pattern). Aesthetically speaking, 'character' is often conferred to an individual koi by very distinctive markings, particularly on the head.

Specific Kohaku Patterns

As discussed in the introduction chapter, various specific Kohaku patterns have been 'fashionable' during the evolution of this type of koi: take, for example, inazuma (lightening stripe) Kohaku, or maruten Kohaku with a separate, often round head pattern. Nevertheless, the classical stepped patterns have maintained their popularity over the years.

Very unusual Kohaku, for example the kanoko (dappled fawn), are classified with Kawarigoi. Kanoko koi have hi as a pattern either completely or partially confined to individual scale areas, giving a reticulated effect (or vignette). Kanoko Kohaku have a delicate appeal, but cannot compete with fairness against more usually patterned Kohaku in official contests.

Gotenzakura and kin-zakura are extremely rare forms of Kohaku. They are said to have small groups of scales involved in each hi marking, like cherry blossoms; those of kin-zakura have golden borders.

Examined in detail, as a group, Kohaku are koi of surprising complexity, considering their deceptively simple red and white colours.

2 Taisho Sanke

Taisho Sanke at a Glance

This is basically a white koi with red (hi) and black (sumi) patterns. Sumi does not usually appear on the head. Body sumi may appear as either tsubo sumi (on the white skin) or kasane sumi (on the hi). Sumi markings are more common above the lateral line. Aka Sanke refers to a Taisho Sanke with almost no visible white skin.

Taisho Sanke	(hi patterns are named as for Kohaku)
Aka Sanke	(hi covers almost the entire head and body)

Not Classified with Taisho Sanke for Show Purposes

	Show Class
Yamatonishiki (metallic Sanke)	Hikarimoyo
Heisei Nishiki (doitsu metallic Sanke)	Hikarimoyo
Kin-Gin-Rin Sanke	Kin-Gin-Rin
Tsubaki Sanke	Kawarigoi

Features

Hi patterns named as for Kohaku (i.e. nidan, sandan, maruten)

Tsubo sumi	'Well-placed' or 'critical', sumi, usually, over white skin.
Kasane sumi	Black pattern over hi.
Tejima or tezumi	Sumi stripes in the finnage.
Aizumi	'Blue' sumi (high-quality).

Taisho Sanke

Urushizumi	'Best sumi', dark and glossy with a hint of blue.
Kurozumi	Rich, glossy black with no blue highlights.
Ato sumi	Late-appearing sumi.
Jari sumi	Gravel sumi, very small spots.
Kokesuki	Colourless scale-sized areas within a pattern element.
Doitsu	Either kagamigoi, having rows of large scales along the dorsal and lateral lines only; or kawagoi, having almost no scales at all.

Introduction

It is probable that Taisho Sanke, together with Kohaku and Showa constitute the three best known and most widely represented koi varieties. The name 'Sanke' means tricolour, this variety being a principally white-skinned fish with red (hi) and black (sumi) markings.

Evolution

The prefix 'Taisho' represents the Japanese era when these koi were first identified (1912–1926) from natural Kohaku mutations, when black spots appeared on some of the offspring. A very few of these three-coloured koi were bred back to Kohaku, resulting in the earliest 'true' Sanke. Eisaburo Hoshino is credited with producing the first recognized Sanke in 1917. Before the prefix 'Taisho', Sanke were called 'Shima' because of the striped finnage

Bloodlines

It is reported that direct Sanke bloodlines may be traced back to only a very few parent stock. The major lineages are Torazo (established around 1949), Sadazo (early 1950s), Jinbei (late 1950s) and Kichinai (early 1960s). The later Izumiya line is said to have been founded from Jinbei stock in the 1970s and early 1980s. Characteristics of these specific bloodlines are still recognizable in modern koi: for

'Doris', a Matsunosuke Sanke, the only koi to have won the BKKS (UK) National Show three times (1997, 1998 and 2000).

This modern Sanke shows a simple but pleasing hi (nidan) pattern, and small neat sumi markings.

example, the very glossy, large sumi markings of Jinbei Sanke, or the 'tiger stripes' of sumi crossing the back, credited to the Torazo Sanke line. However, since breeding other varieties of koi may also produce Sanke – for example, Showa spawnings – there is some scepticism that any 'true-blooded' Sanke remains.

In the 1990s, Matsunosuke and Dainichi Sanke are probably the most representative bloodlines known. Both have excellent growth characteristics; a good, although quite differently shaped figure; and clear, well coloured skin with deep hi and dense sumi. Matsunosuke Sanke tend to mature very late, at about five years or older, but they hold their condition for much longer than many bloodlines. Their sumi often remains below the surface during their early life (ato sumi), making their appearance more like Kohaku.

Dainichi breed superb Sanke and Kohaku, with strong, very graceful lines to their shape. They mature early, and so the fair skin on large, young Dainichi koi provides a natural advantage. It is, perhaps, an indication of the regard in which these Sanke bloodlines are held, that a very large number of other breeders have attempted to incorporate the characteristics of these lines into their own programmes.

Basic Principles of Appreciation

A good starting point to the appreciation of Sanke is to remember that, without the sumi, you should have an excellent Kohaku. All the factors vital to appreciating Kohaku, explored fully in the preceding chapter, are equally important to Sanke, as well as the universal koi appreciation points of good body conformation, high skin quality and an active deportment with well displayed, clear finnage.

In summary, to be truly imposing a Sanke must possess pure white, unblemished skin with a smooth, lustrous appearance. Hi should be solid, even and brightly coloured, in a balanced, well defined, sharp-edged pattern, as for Kohaku. Hi only, should be present on the head of a Sanke, the classical pattern being a U-shape (kutsubera or shoehorn), reaching halfway down the head between the eyes and the nose.

Maruten (separate head pattern) Sanke have been very popular over the years, and non-symmetrical, highly individual 'beret' patterns covering just one side of the head are now considered to be attractive. With a pattern of this kind, however, it is important to remember that the eye should not be stained with hi, and it must also have a clear white rim to escape the heavy appearance that this style of pattern can sometimes confer.

The arrangement of hi on the head of this Sanke is charming. Sumi and hi on the body give a balanced impression.

The shoulder sumi on this doitsu Sanke has great depth. Unfortunately the hi is not strong and the bald head is undesirable, although the large white dorsal area does add necessary balance.

The 'Picasso Sanke', demonstrating more traditionally styled, large sumi markings.

A high quality Sanke without shoulder sumi.

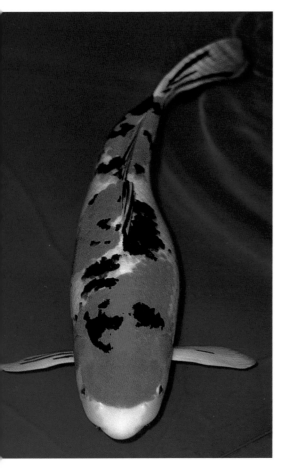

Left: *Sashi is undesirable where black (sumi) overlays red (hi).*

Right: *A good example of a modern Sanke.*

Sanke Sumi

The addition of sumi to the basic red and white pattern gives an extra element to appreciation, and the added interest and challenge to achieving excellence that the third colour component imposes has made Sanke even more popular than Kohaku with many koi keepers.

The quality of the sumi on a Sanke is a vital appreciation point. Originally, its appearance was quite different from that of a Showa (basically, a black koi with red and white): traditional Sanke sumi tended to look painted on, like a layer of thick black lacquer – or 'stepping stones over snow and fire' – whereas Showa sumi seems rather to emerge from within the koi: the former more superficial, seeming to be 'floated' on, the latter more intrinsic to the skin. However, in recent years, koi breeders have attempted to improve the quality of Sanke sumi, which has involved including Showa in some of the breeding programmes. This has resulted in many modern Sanke with sumi of much higher quality, as was intended, but also with greater depth of impression, more in the Showa style, which has caused some classification difficulties at shows in recent years.

Position and Shape

Sanke sumi, unlike that of Showa, is more usually confined to the back of the koi above the lateral line with, traditionally, no sumi appearing anywhere on the head or as pectoral fin joints (motoguro). Sumi markings on the body are often rounded and historically much smaller than those of Showa. Recent breeding programmes however, have resulted in some Sanke lines undergoing a dramatic change in the appearance of their sumi patterns, as well as in sumi quality, with often larger, more angular body markings, sumi occasionally appearing on the head and, confusingly, even as motoguro.

The size and position of sumi markings are unique to each koi and often change radically during the life of a Sanke depending on both genetic factors and keeping conditions.

Colour

Sumi should always look deep black, glossy and solid. Scaling should not be visible through the black pigment, and the edges of the markings should be sharp, particularly the trailing edge (kiwa). Although it may be almost impossible to distinguish between some of them, there are several basic shades of sumi, of which aizumi (blue sumi) from the Asagi Magoi line is thought to be the most desirable. Others are urushizumi (black with a hint of blue), kurozumi (black only) and nabe sumi (greyish and undeveloped).

This Sanke shows rather extreme sumi: it dominates the koi.

Sumi is described as either tsubo ('well-placed' sumi or sumi in a critical postion to the pattern), which generally superimposes white skin, or kasane sumi, overlapping hi. Sumi bordered by white looks very elegant, having a high impact. White skin offset by black also tends to look even whiter, especially if a little bluish sashi borders the leading edges of the sumi markings, giving greater depth. Kasane sumi, considered less stable than tsubo sumi, does not provide the same contrast, overlaying red, although if the marking are large and well-defined the effect is imposing. Kasane sumi should not demonstrate sashi, as this may indicate a thin hi plate

Pattern

Sumi on the body of a Sanke is thought to begin, ideally, with a large marking on the shoulder – although it must be recognized that this is merely a preference, and not a 'standard'. There are no laid-down breed standards in koi appreciation, as there are for horses or dogs, for example, since there are just too many variables involved; thus many perfectly acceptable and very elegant Sanke occur without a shoulder sumi marking.

There is no definitive Sanke sumi pattern either, although a 'chequerboard' style of well defined sumi markings along either side of the back of the koi always gives a very pleasing impression; but this must work with the hi pattern at the same time. It is impossible to look at any element in a pattern

An Aka Sanke will show a line between hi and white on some portion of the head or body.

On a doitsu koi, pattern elements must look particularly sharp to be competitive with those of fully scaled contemporaries.

A Sanke of outstanding quality. Note the fukurin, or reticulated effect, over white skin.

truly in isolation. Balance of both hi and sumi, in proportion to white skin, is important from side to side of the koi, as well as head to tail. A common problem is a 'front-ended' hi pattern in conjunction with sumi that is largely concentrated near the tail end of the koi. Another problem is where large numbers of very small spots of sumi (jari or gravel sumi) speckle the skin: this tends to look untidy and unattractive, like tobi hi.

Sumi and Finnage

Sumi often appears in Sanke finnage, and ideally should be seen as a very few light stripes. Early Sanke were typified by very heavily striped finnage, though today this is not recognized as a desirable feature. Some stripes, however, are thought to demonstrate the presence of a true bloodline and stable body sumi. Plain white finnage is very elegant, and certainly does not exclude a Sanke from being appreciated, however it may point to it having a lineage recently crossbred with Kohaku. Black fin joints (motoguru) should not be present, since these are prerequisites of Showa.

Styles of Sanke

In the same way as for Kohaku, preferred styles of Sanke have altered over the years according to popular demand. An overall trend for very many years, however, has been towards a reduction of the amount of sumi present and a lighter style of Sanke. The culmination of this trend was the so-called 'minimum Sanke' with only a single, or very few small sumi markings visible. From the mid-1990s, however, there has been an increasing return to appreciation of larger, denser sumi markings in the Jinbei style, although without the accompanying heavily striped finnage.

A colour variant, the red (aka) Sanke is also popular. Almost no white skin is visible from above, although somewhere there will be a solid line between the red and white skin, over the nose, near the tail or below the lateral line. If the hi is strong and even and the sumi large and impressive, these koi can look very imposing, even though three appreciation points are lost – namely the impact of sumi against white skin, the hi pattern and the edges of the hi.

In Conclusion

Achieving a really top class Sanke is even more difficult than it is for Kohaku, where there are only two colour variables in the equation. Hence it is vital that a koi's good points be always sought first. It is too easy to dismiss a worthy koi on demerits. There will always be some imperfections. When appreciating Sanke, look for the overall harmony of the three colours, their relative depth, and the size and position of the pattern elements compared with the size of the koi. The way in which the interaction of the figure, skin quality, colour and patterns work together is truly fascinating, and different for every individual koi.

3 Showa Sanshoku

Showa Sanshoku at a Glance

A Showa is a three-coloured koi (black, white and red), originally thought of as 'black-based' due to the large proportion of sumi displayed by traditional Showa. Four characteristics of the original patterning are still used to distinguish Showa from Sanke today:

1. Sumi is usually present on the head, and particularly the nose, of a Showa. Typical patterning is either as a 'v' (or inverted Japanese Kanji symbol) on the forehead with a separate nose sumi, or as a 'lightening stripe' (menware or hachiware) dividing the head.
2. Sumi on the body of a Showa tends to wrap around, over the back, reaching below the lateral line, often in highly asymmetrical, jagged-looking patterns. Sumi may also appear in large blocks.
3. Sumi on the pectoral fins of a Showa appears as black fin joints (motoguro) rather than as stripes in the fins.
4. Sumi appears inside the mouth of a Showa.

Any one or combination of these characteristics tends to distinguish Showa from Sanke in the majority of cases. Two variants may be seen: Kage Showa, that has a shadowed look to the white skin with solid sumi and red (hi) patterns; and Boke Showa that has grey, or grey and black unfinished-looking sumi.

Traditional Showa	(approximately 30 per cent white skin)
Kindai Showa	(modern Showa with a much larger proportion of white skin)
Boke Showa	(blurred sumi, unfinished appearance)
Hi Showa	(almost no visible white skin, at first glance a red and black koi)
Kage Showa	(white skin appears shadowed)

Not Classified as Showa Sanshoku for Show Purposes:

	Show Class
Kin Showa (metallic Showa)	Hikari Utsuri
Kanoko Showa (dappled hi)	Kawarigoi
Kin-Gin-Rin Showa (rows of very shiny scales along the back and sides of the koi)	Kin–Gin–Rin
Koromo Showa (scale reticulations over the hi)	Koromo in the UK, or Koromo or Kawarigoi using the ZNA classification

Features

Motoguro	Black pectoral fin joints.
Menware or Hachiware	Lightening stripe head sumi.
Hanazumi	Sumi on the nose.
Nabe sumi	Greyish sumi from the Tetsu Magoi line.
Kutchizumi	Sumi on the lips.
Doitsu	Either kagamigoi, having rows of large scales along the dorsal and lateral lines only, or kawagoi having almost no scales at all.

Introduction

Showa were originally described as black-skinned koi, with superimposed red (hi) and white patterns. Together with Kohaku (a white koi with red markings) and Sanke (a white koi with red and black markings), they are the third of the so-called 'big three' show varieties of koi. Today it is perhaps a little simplistic to think of either Showa or Utsurimono (originally a black koi with one other colour, namely white, red or yellow) as basically black, since modern koi of these varieties have very large proportions of white skin. It is better to think of them as koi demonstrating (usually) at least two

out of the following criteria (although, as always with koi, there are exceptions):

- The head, and particularly the nose, develop sumi (black).
- The pectoral fins have black joints (motoguro).
- Sumi on the body of the koi is arranged in either 'mountain-shaped' blocks on either side of the dorsal fin, reaching up from well below the lateral line (the traditional style), or is present as 'jagged lightening', narrow, asymmetrical markings across the back and well down the flanks.
- Sumi is present in the mouth.

It has been said that if it is impossible to classify a Showa from the external appearance, they will usually have sumi inside the mouth.

Evolution

The first Showa was bred in the 1920s: it is credited to Mr Jukichi Hoshino, who is said to have crossed a Ki Utsuri (Utsuri with yellow markings) with a Kohaku. Ki Utsuri appeared from the Tetsu (iron) Magoi line, and characteristics of these carp still occur in modern Showa. The so-called nabe sumi (grey and undeveloped sumi) that gives a kage (shadowed) effect is attributed to the original Tetsu

A classic Showa with all three colours in similar proportions. White is crisp, hi and sumi are very homogeneous. The nose sumi adds character to this koi.

The Kindai Showa has a much higher proportion of white skin. The sumi in this case is still not fully developed.

Although the sumi on this high quality koi is unbalanced, the heavier hi on the opposite side works well as a counterbalance, providing high impact.

Right: A Showa demonstrating an attractive vignette effect over some of the sumi.

Magoi. The rich, velvety, dense black sumi, so desirable for high quality Showa, owes its origins to the Asagi Magoi line of koi.

Early Showa had very yellow hi and poor quality white skin. In the 1940s Mr Tomiji Kobayashi created the famous Kobayashi Showa with deep red hi by crossbreeding existing Showa with Yagozen Kohaku; this established the line that led to modern Showa. Refinement has continued since that time, as well as considerable effort to produce a more imposing shape: Kobayashi Showa were originally very slender koi with poor growth characteristics.

Modern Showa

It was not until the 1960s that modern (kindai) Showa began to appear, demonstrating far more white skin due to the continued crossbreeding with other high quality bloodlines, for example Tomoin Kohaku. This has ultimately resulted in the superb, extensive hi and white being seen in Showa today. However, they still do not readily achieve the size gained by koi of other varieties. It is reported that, particularly, Dainichi are working very hard to improve the growth of Showa while maintaining the level of quality which has taken so many years to reach.

Unfortunately, Showa crossed with Showa do not breed true, numbers produced are much lower – only about 30 per cent of any spawning – than other varieties, and a supreme quality Showa is probably the most difficult koi to find. Good quality Showa are also the most difficult to maintain, since a Showa's appearance can change dramatically during its lifespan. This fact does add a certain piquancy to their appreciation, since it is always a bit of a gamble as to whether your Showa stays the same, improves, or rapidly becomes something you would like to auction off anonymously. (The author will accept offers for a koi of the latter style currently living in her pond.)

Basic Principles of Showa Appreciation

To appreciate Showa the basic principles governing all koi must be applied first. The koi must possess a good frame, that is, it must be well proportioned from head to tail and bilaterally. Finnage should be clean-looking, smooth-edged and in proportion to the size of the koi. High quality skin should appear lustrous, with glowing, bright hi, glossy, ebony sumi and pure,

A stunning combination of bright white, deep hi, jet-black sumi and some areas of kage scaling.

A very traditionally styled Hi Showa. The extensive, high quality sumi gives a powerful impression.

A Kindai Showa that at first glance emulates a Sanke. Closer examination reveals the typical jagged, deep-wrapping Showa-style sumi and small motoguru on the pectoral fins.

Showa Sanshoku

Right: *A very unusual doitsu koi. The sumi on the nose and belly classify this koi as Showa.*

Below: *Sumi on a Showa usually wraps deeply around the body.*

translucent white markings. The koi should be alert, in balance, and free swimming with well displayed finnage. It is important to remember that large areas of black skin, typical for Showa, can hide defects of conformation quite effectively. This is particularly true when the sumi extends over a part of the koi that curves out of sight, for example the cheeks or nose. Conversely, sumi in this area may make a perfectly well proportioned head look too small.

Showa Sumi

The quality and positioning of the sumi on a Showa are vital appreciation points. Ideally, sumi markings should look well defined, very solid and shiny. Kiwa – the trailing edge of the sumi element – should be crisply outlined, with no sumi speckles bleeding into white- or red-patterned areas. Sumi should also give the impression of great depth, of emerging from within the body, and of being overlaid by the other pattern components.

Interestingly, Showa often demonstrate areas of sumi that are grey rather than black, or show a vignette effect of white within the sumi. If well defined and combined with areas of dense black sumi, these variations are very beautiful and add to, rather than detract from the overall impression of the koi. Modern patterns are often highly asymmetrical, which also adds to the high level of individuality that this variety demonstrates.

Head Patterns

The head of a Showa is expected to possess sumi. Two patterns are common: a lightening stripe (menware or hashiware) dividing the head lengthways; or a 'v' shape on the forehead (an upside-down Japanese Kanji character), with or without nose sumi (hanazumi). Other variations occur besides these, and are quite acceptable as long as they are balanced. Ideally hi and white should harmonize with sumi on the head of a Showa to create a beautiful design. Particularly, white skin bordering the eyes and on the nose creates a very clean impression and allows fuller appreciation of these features.

Finnage

Black fin joints (motoguro) are not essential, but they do add a positive appreciation point if well balanced. The black pigment should not extend more than a third of the length of the fin, although additional small stripes extending from the motoguro in a starburst pattern may look very attractive on a large koi. Remember, very heavy motoguro seen on one- and two-year-old koi (tosai, nesai, respectively) will often regress to classic neat fin joints with time.

Sumi should not dominate any part of a Showa, although it must still be obvious and eye-catching. A useful guideline is that equal amounts of all three pattern components are thought desirable.

Colour and Skin Quality

The white markings on a traditionally marked Showa only comprised up to 30 per cent of the skin surface. For a Showa, it is more important to have high quality white skin in small quantities than large areas that are yellowish or stained. In recent years the quality of the white may be expected to equal that found on traditionally 'white-based' koi such as Kohaku and Sanke. Placing of the white markings has no specific recommendation, although it does depend for effect on the position of the two other colour components. However, a pure white marking before the tail, following the last hiban and matching a white nose, is both highly desirable and looks exceptionally elegant.

Kindai Showa

In recent years Showa with a higher proportion of white skin have been selected for. These modern (Kindai) Showa have developed because many people feel that both hi and sumi patterns look more attractive when adjacent to white skin. The situation now is that many Kindai Showa are barely distinguishable from Sanke without very close examination, since they may have no more sumi than an average Sanke. This problem has been

A Hi Showa of much lighter style.

A rare and excellent example of a doitsu Hi Showa.

exacerbated by the recent appearance of Sanke with 'Showa-style' sumi, described in the previous chapter. However, a very close examination of the quality, position and shape of the black markings usually results in the correct show classification of these two varieties.

While Kindai Showa are undeniably attractive, elegant and often quite stunning with their high proportion of snowy white skin offsetting hi and sumi markings, they are 'lighter' in style and lack the compelling power given by more extensive coal black, glossy sumi in the more traditional style.

Hi Quality and Patterns for Showa

These are essentially as prescribed for Kohaku, explored fully in the chapter dedicated to that variety. In summary, the red colour must be strong, even, and ideally, thick enough to make scaling almost invisible. The trailing edges of hi elements should be sharp, and the pattern itself should extend in a balanced fashion along the whole length of the back. The head should possess some hi.

A Showa having a straight (ippon) hi, with almost no white skin visible from head to tail when viewed from above, is called a Hi Showa and is a popular variant. Although Hi Showa may look very impressive, it is generally thought that they lack a certain elegance when compared to a more obviously tricoloured Showa.

In Conclusion

As we have seen, Showa present many problems for the hobbyist. They generally tend to have poor growth characteristics; their heads are often pointed and may appear too short; and deformities are more common for this variety than many others. They also seem to be rather weak with respect to health (certainly in the author's experience), perhaps due to intensive line breeding. Regarding pattern, hi is often confined to the head end of the koi, while the tail end is too heavily marked with sumi. Sumi itself is often blurred and light (boke) and never develops fully, a great frustration when potentially the sumi markings are excellently placed.

The list of potential problems coupled to the few numbers actually bred gives some idea as to why a top quality Showa is rare.

Finally, Showa are noble looking, powerful, dramatic and enigmatic koi, and it is always a privilege to see a really superb example whether it is a traditional, Hi or Kindai Showa variation.

4 Utsurimono

Utsurimono at a Glance

This is a two-coloured koi, originally thought of as 'black-based' due to the large proportion of sumi displayed by traditional Utsurimono. The second colour may be white, red or, very rarely, yellow. Four characteristics of the original sumi patterning are still used to distinguish Utsurimono from other black and white koi (Bekko and Karasugoi) today; these are as follows:

1. Sumi is usually present on the head, and particularly the nose, of an Utsurimono. Typical patterning is either as a 'v' (or inverted Japanese Kanji symbol) on the forehead with a separate nose sumi, or as a 'lightening stripe' (menware or hachiware) dividing the head.
2. Sumi on the body of an Utsurimono tends to wrap around, over the back, reaching below the lateral line, often in highly asymmetrical, jagged-looking patterns. It may also appear in large blocks.
3. Sumi on the pectoral fins of an Utsurimono appears as black fin joints (motoguro) rather than as stripes in the fins.
4. Sumi appears inside the mouth.

Any one or combination of these characteristics tends to distinguish Utsurimono from Bekko (a white/red/yellow-based' koi with black markings) in the majority of cases.

Kage Utsuri, like Kage Showa, have a shadowed finish to white, red or yellow skin.

Shiro Utsuri	(black and white)
Hi Utsuri	(black and red)
Ki Utsuri	(black and yellow)
Gin-Rin Shiro Utsuri	(rows of very shiny silver scales along the back and sides of the koi)
Kin-Rin Hi or Ki Utsuri	(rows of very shiny golden scales along the back and sides of the koi)

Utsurimono

Not Classified as Utsurimono for Show Purposes

	Show Class
Kage Utsuri (shadowed white, red or yellow skin)	Kawarigoi
Gin Shiro Utsuri (metallic Shiro Utsuri)	Hikari Utsuri
Kin Ki Utsuri (metallic Ki Utsuri)	Hikari Utsuri
Kin Hi Utsuri (metallic Hi Utsuri)	Hikari Utsuri

Features

Motoguro	Black pectoral fin joints.
Menware or Hachiware	Lightening stripe head sumi
Hanazumi	Sumi on the nose.
Nabe sumi	Greyish sumi from the Tetsu Magoi line.
Kutchizumi	Sumi on the lips.
Doitsu	Either kagamigoi, having rows of large scales along the dorsal and lateral lines only, or kawagoi having almost no scales at all.

Introduction

Like Showa, Utsurimono were traditionally said to be 'black-based', but are two-coloured koi rather than three-coloured. The class comprises three colour variants, the best known being the Shiro Utsuri (black with white patterns), followed by Hi Utsuri (black with red patterns).

The third colour variant is Ki Utsuri (black with yellow patterns), now a koi very rarely seen, although it was the first Utsuri type to be recognized.

Evolution

Ki Utsuri are, in fact, amongst the earliest of any known nishikigoi, having been first described in the Meiji era in the late nineteenth century; at this time it is said they were called 'Kuro Ki Han', meaning 'black and yellow markings'. The original breeder of this variety of koi was Mr Eizaburo Hoshino, who stabilized it in 1920 from the Tetsu Magoi line, and it appears that he was responsible for giving it the name 'Ki Utsuri'.

Shiro Utsuri are recorded as being first bred as a stable line by Mr Kazuo Minemura in 1925, and of the three Utsurimono variants it has proved to be by far the most popular. The word 'Utsuri' indicates change or reflection, referring to the tendency for the sumi of this variety to alter radically during early development.

Classification

There are three black and white varieties of nishikigoi: Shiro Utsuri, Shiro Bekko and the Karasugoi, classified with Kawarigoi. Of the three, Karasugoi are very different in appearance: their sumi is usually far more extensive than that of either Shiro Utsuri or Shiro Bekko, the whole body of the koi often being black (i.e. Hajiro, Hageshiro). Where white skin is visible on the body of a Karasugoi, the sumi markings are usually arranged laterally, streaming from head to tail rather than from side to side over the back, as they do for Shiro Utsuri. In the Karasu group sumi may also appear as a full black and white vignette (Suminagashi), or as a changing pattern of black and white where the two colours dominate either the head or the tail end of the koi, according to time and season (Matsukawabake).

Although the Karasugoi are thus (generally) easily recognizable, a common problem for inexperienced hobbyists is to confuse Shiro Utsuri with Shiro Bekko, traditionally a 'white-based' koi with more rounded black patterns on the body in the Sanke style. In distinguishing between Shiro Utsuri and Bekko there are four main points to remember:

- Shiro Bekko are mostly white and generally do not have any black markings on the head, although occasionally small spots do occur. Shiro Utsuri are expected to have a distinctive black head pattern, which tends to include sumi on the nose.
- The black markings on the body of a Bekko tend to be confined to the back, above the lateral line. Utsuri sumi usually wraps extensively round the body.
- The shape and quality of the black markings on a Bekko are usually quite different to those on Utsuri, being more rounded and 'floating', as opposed to irregular and angular, and giving the impression of emerging from within the skin.
- Utsuri, traditionally 'black-based' like Showa, tend to have sumi inside the mouth.

A Kumonryu (Kawarigoi), *showing the lateral 'head-to-tail' arrangement of sumi.*

A high quality, modern Shiro Utsuri.

Appearance

Tremendous effort has been put into improving particularly Shiro Utsuri in recent years, with quite spectacular results; the quality of this variety of koi is now reaching an eminently high standard. Intensive work on the part of the breeders of Utsuri has resulted in exceptional 'blue-white' skin and wonderful blue-black, high quality, lustrous sumi that is considerably more stable and less likely to scatter as jari sumi (gravel). Like Showa, however, Utsurimono do not grow well, so do not readily achieve jumbo proportions.

Utsurimono originally demonstrated far more black skin than white, red or yellow, and the finnage was very dark; all this tended to give a rather gloomy impression, despite it being a powerful and often dramatic combination. Early Shiro Utsuri often had red pigment under the black, resulting in a brownish-black sumi instead of the more desirable blue-black finish. However, although small red areas still occasionally appear on the skin of Shiro Utsuri, this problem has largely been bred out, and sumi on modern Utsurimono, and particularly on Shiro Utsuri, is

Like Showa, Utsurimono demonstrates boke scaling during the development of the sumi.

The sashi of Shiro Utsuri provides a 'blue-white' finish to the white skin.

A mature Shiro Utsuri which shows some yellowing of the white skin.

A traditional Shiro Utsuri has approximately equal proportions of black and white skin.

very refined. However, greyish nabe sumi, a legacy of the original line from Tetsu Magoi, is still sometimes seen on modern Utsurimono.

Basic Principles of Utsurimono Appreciation

When appreciating Utsurimono, the starting point, as always, is a well conformed koi: this means that the overall proportions of head, body and finnage should be balanced and symmetrical. This, basic but absolutely essential requirement for a sound conformation, is closely followed by the need for excellent skin quality and an alert deportment, with well displayed finnage.

Shiro Utsuri

For a koi of such stark and simple black and white marking, the high skin quality of today's Shiro Utsuri produces an incredibly beautiful and eye-catching result. Dense, velvety, blue-black sumi is offset by snowy white, and this very cool white finish is enhanced even more by the deep blue sashi that often rims the leading edge of each sumi marking.

The trailing edge (kiwa), on the other hand, is required to be sharply defined, and a common problem is that the sumi kiwa is insufficiently clear cut. Generally, the kiwa of Utsurimono sumi is in the kamisori or razor border style, cutting across scales; however, is has recently been indicated that work is in progress to produce Showa and Utsuri with maruzome, or scalloped kiwa of sumi. Modern sumi patterns often show a highly asymmetrical, 'jagged lightening' effect that is breeder dependent. White skin is often very extensive, and makes a stunning combination with the artistry of this type of sumi arrangement.

Shiro Utsuri of more traditional style have more sumi, often arranged in a symmetrical, square 'chequerboard' (ichimatsu) pattern along the back, or as 'mountain peaks' rising from the belly of the koi to the dorsal line.

Skin Quality

Contemporarily, selection towards the breeding of Shiro Utsuri with a higher percentage of white skin is very common; as with Showa, the appeal of the modern, lighter style has predominated. The quality of the white skin in Shiro Utsuri has achieved a very high grade, and may be expected to be a smooth, glossy, unstained and very pure white. Likewise the sumi markings should be solid ebony, or blue-black throughout, with no visible scaling. The deep blue sashi that slightly blurs the leading edges is thought to confer a three-dimensional effect, and so enhance the appearance of the white skin: it is therefore a desirable feature on Shiro Utsuri. Very small sumi speckles spreading into the white skin should be minimal: these were a very real problem to early breeders of this variety, but the tendency for them to appear has largely been overcome.

Pattern

The pattern of black and white markings is required only to show balance, although it is considered elegant if a black marking on the head is matched on the same side at the tail with white. Highly variable styles may impart an equally pleasing impression and are very much "demand led" in their appearance. Black fin joints (motoguro) on the pectoral fins are not essential for appreciation, but are thought to point towards the presence of good quality, stable sumi. Very extensive motoguro on young koi (tosai, nisei) tends to regress as the koi ages. Sumi on Utsurimono becomes stable after about four or five years.

Head Pattern
The head usually demonstrates some sumi. Traditional head patterns are the same as those for Showa, either a sumi stripe bisecting the head (menware or hashiware) or a forehead 'v' shape

Head patterns of modern Shiro Utsuri are both delicate and highly attractive.

A Hi Utsuri with lovely deep hi, but the black pectorals give a heavy impression and kiwa of sumi is very poor.

51

This Ki Utsuri demonstrates the common problems of heavy sumi over head and finnage, and breakage of the kiwa with speckling over the yellow base colour.

with separate nose sumi. However, such an arrangement is by no means essential for appreciation, since there are no prescribed 'standards' for patterns in koi. Very unusual head patterns are now seen on Utsurimono with charming effect. Modern Shiro Utsuri may also, acceptably, demonstrate very minimal sumi on their heads. It is important only that head and body patterns work together in the proportion and style of black and white skin, together creating an artistically pleasing balance.

Hi Utsuri

Hi (red) Utsuri have also been very popular over the years, the black and red colours making a powerful contrast. Unfortunately, good quality Hi Utsuri are very rare since they are not specifically bred for, but only appear from time to time in other spawnings,

for example from those of Showa; but when discovered, they are capable of competing at the highest level. The hi should be thick and homogeneous, ideally a bright, orange-based red; however, the homogeneity of the colour is more important than the actual shade of red, and this is difficult to achieve.

A major problem with Hi Utsuri is the instability of the sumi kiwa, with consequent spreading of tiny sumi speckles across the red skin; this produces an untidy, unfinished look. Also the sumi markings are often of poor quality, giving a 'washed out' appearance. Distribution of the sumi tends to be uneven, too predominant at the head or tail, or along one side. The pectoral fins, unlike Shiro Utsuri and Showa, tend to be heavily striped with sumi, rather than having neat motoguro. Nevertheless, when combined with a completely red fin, these stripes look very attractive, especially on a large koi. There is a tendency, however, for Hi Utsuri to have completely black finnage, which again, gives a heavy appearance.

Utsurimono often demonstrate very individual patterns.

Perhaps the rarity of good Hi Utsuri has promoted hobbyists towards collecting Aka Sanke and Hi Showa, both essentially red and black koi – admittedly not quite the same, but more readily available at an acceptable quality. Theoretically, a top quality Hi Utsuri should be as clean-looking as a Shiro Utsuri in its arrangement of hi and sumi. This is almost never achieved, however.

Ki Utsuri

Ki Utsuri are very similar to Hi Utsuri on all points except the second colour, which should be a bright yellow, even and unstained. Colour on the pectoral fins may shade acceptably to white at the tips. Sadly this highly attractive variety is almost never seen, perhaps because of the difficulty in stabilizing the sumi markings. The metallic equivalent of Ki Utsuri (Kin Ki Utsuri) is relatively common in the UK.

Examining this koi gives an insight to the potential beauty of the combination of non-metallic black and yellow skin.

In Conclusion

Utsurimono are a high-impact group, providing a powerful and vigorous first impression, their fascinating pattern asymmetry is vivid and highly individual. They are living proof that the attractiveness and character of a koi depend on more than excellent shape and skin, and that it is the way in which the pattern components are put together that can make or break the impression. Furthermore, although abstract factors such as distinction and elegance, 'chic' and dignity are difficult to evaluate, they are nonetheless vital components of koi appreciation.

5 Bekko

Bekko at a Glance

Shiro Bekko are white koi with black (sumi) patterns. Unlike the 'black-based' Utsurimono, the sumi patterns are more rounded in appearance and usually occur above the lateral line. Bekko do not have black pectoral fin joints, and rarely show any sumi on the head (and never on the nose). Two Bekko variants are the Aka Bekko, red with black; and the very rare Ki Bekko, yellow with black.

Shiro Bekko	(white with black patterns)
Aka Bekko	(red with black patterns. Note: finnage may be white)
Ki Bekko	(yellow with black patterns)
Kin-Gin-Rin Shiro / Aka / Ki Bekko	(rows of very shiny scales along the back and sides of the koi)

Not Classified with Bekko for Show Purposes

	Show Class
Gin Shiro Bekko (metallic Shiro Bekko)	Hikarimoyo
Tora Ogon (metallic Ki Bekko)	Hikarimoyo

Features

Doitsu	Either kagamigoi, having rows of large scales along the dorsal and lateral lines only, or kawagoi having almost no scales at all.
Tegima or Tezumi	Sumi stripes in the finnage.

Aizumi	'Blue' sumi.
Urushizumi	'Best sumi,' dark and glossy with a hint of blue.
Kurozumi	Rich, glossy black sumi, no blue highlights.
Ato Sumi	Late-appearing sumi.

Introduction

Bekko (literally tortoiseshell) are either, white (Shiro), red (Aka) or yellow (Ki) koi with black (sumi) markings. The Ki Bekko is now very rare. Shiro Bekko are most commonly seen, and although Aka Bekko are popular, few are produced. The earliest Bekko are said to have appeared in the Taisho era, 1912–1926.

Evolution

Considerable confusion appears to exist over the early genealogy of Bekko as a variety of koi. Shiro Bekko are thought to originate from Taisho Sanke (white with red and black markings) lineage, since reference is made to both Shiro and Aka Bekko arising from the introduction of Kohaku (white with red markings) and Ai-goromo (white with blue reticulated red markings) to Sanke breeding programmes. Aka and Ki Bekko are also variously said to have been originally produced from a Higoi (original red, single-coloured koi)/Magoi (wild carp) cross, or from continually crossbreeding Tetsu (iron) Magoi that carry genes for both black and red. Today, most Bekko are a 'by-product' of Sanke breeding programmes, hence their rarity.

Appearance and Recognition

As mentioned in the last chapter, confusion of Shiro Bekko and Shiro Utsuri is a common problem for beginners, as is the correct recognition of Aka Bekko and Aka Sanke. Think of a Shiro Bekko as being a Taisho Sanke without the red (hi) markings. All the attributes applying to the position of white and black skin on a Sanke also relate to Bekko.

- Sumi on the body is largely confined above the lateral line. Markings tend to be discrete, smaller and more rounded than those of Showa ('black-based', with red and white) or Utsurimono ('black-based' with one other colour, white, red, or yellow).
- It is unusual to see sumi on the head, particularly on the nose area.
- Sumi markings in the pectorals, when present,

appear as light stripes, never as solid wedges on the fin joints (motoguro).
- Sumi inside the mouth is unlikely.

Shiro Utsuri resembles Showa without hi, in the same way:

- Sumi on the body tends to be quite extensive, jagged and dramatic in appearance, and wraps around the whole body.
- Sumi is usually present on the head. A nose marking is common.
- Sumi on the pectorals, when present, originates at the joint as a solid marking (motoguro).
- Sumi is expected inside the mouth.

A Gin-Rin Shiro Bekko of the highest quality.
The white skin is delicate and very clean-looking,
and the sumi markings are small, dense and very neat.

A common problem for Shiro Bekko: a yellow head.

A Shiro Bekko showing extensive blue sashi and a small sumi marking on the head.

At first glance an Aka Sanke may seem indistinguishable from an Aka Bekko; however, somewhere on an Aka Sanke there will be a solid line between red and white skin, either over the nose, near the tail or below the lateral line. Aka Bekko may have a pale belly and white finnage, but nowhere on the head or body will you see a definite line between white and red.

Basic Principles of Bekko Appreciation

To appreciate Bekko, it goes without saying that the 'basic frame' of the koi – shape, proportion of head, body and finnage – must be excellent: it is impossible to produce impressiveness without a sound conformation. Lineage of the koi goes a long way to providing this outstanding basic shape, coupled with good management of environment and feed, topics outside the scope of this book.

A Gin-Rin Shiro Bekko showing extensive, scattered sumi.

Deportment of the koi also plays an important role in how impressive the individual appears. An alert, interested awareness coupled with erect, well displayed fins attracts the eye. Add the impact of the sheer massiveness of a large koi, and you have a powerful impression indeed, irrespective of variety.

The skin should always appear smooth, clear, soft, bright and lustrous. The inability to be able to see individual scale edges is a useful indicator for a high quality skin. Bekko tend to have a very large proportion of base colour, with relatively few sumi markings; hence the intrinsic quality of the skin, whether good or bad, tends to be very obvious.

Shiro Bekko

Shiro Bekko should have a true white base, without any yellowing. Unfortunately, a common problem for Shiro Bekko is the development of a yellow head. The best white is soft and bright, giving a delicate appearance. Modern Shiro Bekko have white skin which tends to give a cool-looking, 'blue-white' impression, due to the presence of deep blue sashi (the leading-edge scale insertion point) often appearing at the beginning of each sumi marking. A clean, all-white head is very attractive, offset by the very bright blue eyes usually seen on Shiro Bekko. A small sumi marking appearing on the forehead, which balances the markings on the body, does not detract from the overall impression.

Sumi

Sumi on the body of a Shiro Bekko can give the appearance of a chequerboard pattern across the back, quite symmetrical, although this is not a requirement for excellence. The comparison to 'stepping stones in the snow' gives a rather more eloquent description of the way in which the pattern of sumi and white interact for this variety. Ideally, markings should be similar in size. A large sumi marking on the shoulder is thought to be desirable, since this balances the broadest part of the koi's body. Many, very small scattered sumi speckles (jari or gravel, goma or sesame sumi) give an untidy look, but overall, the impressiveness of the sumi arises far more from its basic quality than from its arrangement.

Sumi should look jet black, shiny, and solidly well defined, with no individual scales visible within the markings. Traditionally, the impression of sumi was expected to be that of 'floating' on the white ground. Today, however, a very different three-dimensional impact is common, due to the appearance over the last decade of deep blue scale insertions (sashi of sumi) at the leading edges of sumi markings on Shiro Bekko. Where sashi is present, it is important that it looks even, extending only one scale width at the leading edge of each pattern element.

The highest quality sumi is blue based, as for Taisho Sanke. Early Bekko demonstrated extensive, soft nabe sumi from the Tetsu magoi line. Sumi

Above: *A good example of an Aka Bekko. Hi is strongly coloured and sumi markings neat.*

Above: *The clean impression of a Shiro Bekko may be quickly spoiled by skin flushing, due to stress.*

Bekko

A Gin-Rin Shiro Bekko.

quality has been much improved over the years. Today, the sumi of most Bekko is a mixture of honzumi ('hard', indigo black) and nabe sumi. The contrast between lacquer black sumi and pure white skin is an important appreciation point for Shiro Bekko. The impression is completed by a few delicate stripes of sumi appearing in the finnage (tejima or tezumi); these are thought to indicate sumi stability.

Aka Bekko

Aka Bekko should demonstrate the same sumi quality as Shiro Bekko. Hi ground must demonstrate depth, as well as brightness and uniformity of colour, rare on larger koi. Sashi of sumi on Aka Bekko is undesirable, probably indicating a thin hi plate. Like Benigoi (or Higoi – classified in Kawarigoi), another all red koi, the fins may be tipped with white or be almost all white, which makes an attractive contrast with the red body.

Aka Bekko have scarcity value, but tend not to be able to compete in terms of elegance with Shiro Bekko. So much hi can give a rather heavy impression. Ki Bekko has a yellow base with sumi markings, and is now almost extinct as a type. Occasionally its metallic equivalent, Tora Ogon appears, giving a brief reminder of this attractive colour combination.

An outstanding example of a modern Shiro Bekko.

In Search of Excellence

The traditional impact of the Bekko, particularly Shiro Bekko, is one of lightness, neatness and delicate elegance, rather than power. The clean white head with often very bright blue eyes is particularly appealing. Considerable change, however, in the appearance and impression of Shiro Bekko is currently occurring; looking at photographs of this variety from ten to twenty years ago the differences are quite clear. Striping of finnage was much heavier on early examples. Sumi lacked depth, even though the proportion of sumi markings was higher.

In the 1990s quite a diversity to the style of sumi began to appear, often with deep blue, regular sashi giving a much stronger, impressive finish to much larger and more irregular sumi markings, and heightening the blue tone of the white skin. This perhaps stems from the introduction of Showa bloodlines into the Sanke breeding programmes to improve the basic quality of sumi. Additionally, many Bekko with beautiful kin-gin-rin scaling are appearing, a definite enhancement for what has been a rather plain koi.

In Conclusion

Although for sheer drama of impact, the Utsurimono will be difficult to outshine, Bekko is a variety well worth watching over the next few years. A new impressiveness is beginning to be achieved, which may well revitalize a line of koi somewhat neglected by hobbyists over the last decade.

6 Tancho

Tancho at a Glance

A koi with a distinctive, usually round, marking on the head in a colour that does not appear anywhere else on the body. For example, a Kuro Tancho Orenji Ogon is a metallic orange-coloured koi with a black marking only on the head. A red (hi) marking is the most common head pattern colour.

Tancho Kohaku	(a white koi with hi only on the head)
Tancho Sanke	(a 'white-based' koi with black patterns and a hi marking only on the head)
Tancho Showa	(a 'black-based' koi with white patterns and a hi marking only on the head)
Kin-Gin-Rin Tancho Kohaku, Sanke or Showa	(rows of very shiny scales along the back and side of the koi)

Not Classified with Tancho for Show Purposes

	Show Class
Tancho Kujaku (meallic white koi with a vignette or 'pine cone' reticulated pattern over the body and a golden or metallic red marking on the head only. Also called Kin Tancho Gin Matsuba.	Hikarimoyo
Tancho Ogon (metallic white, grey, cream or yellow, with a metallic red marking only on the head)	Hikarimoyo

Tancho Goshiki
(basically red and
white, with blue or
black scale reticulations
over a white body only;
in the case of a tancho,
a hi marking occurs on
the head alone)

Koromo or
Kawarigoi, (ZNA)

Kuro Tancho
(a large black sumi
marking appears only
on the head of the koi.)
These are very rare.
Examples might be
Kuro Tancho Sanke
or Kuro Tancho Ogon

Kawarigoi
Hikarimoyo

Features

Kakutan	Square tancho marking
Umebachi	Tancho marking shaped like the petals of the Japanese apricot tree
Juji	Cross-shaped tancho marking

Above: *Although an attractive Tancho Showa, the edges of the tancho spot show poor definition.*

Introduction

A koi is called a tancho when a particular colour marking, usually red (hi), appears only on the head of the koi. Originally the name was 'Hinomaru', a crimson disk on a white ground, representative of the Japanese national flag.

The word 'tancho' derives from the Japanese crane, a white bird with a round red crest. Any koi variety having more than one colour has the possibility of producing a tancho: for example Tancho Goshiki, a basic red and white koi with shades of blue and black as an overlaying scale reticulated effect, or vignette; or Tancho Ogon, a metallic white, grey, cream or yellow koi with a metallic red marking only on the head. However, tancho koi are more usually associated with Kohaku, a white koi with red patterns; with Taisho Sanke, a 'white-based' koi with red and black; and with Showa Sanshoku, a 'black-based' koi with red and white, differently arranged from Taisho Sanke. It is just these three (Go-Sanke) varieties that provide the characteristic pattern variants that make up the show class Tancho. Other koi having a tancho pattern are classified with their basic variety.

Although a red head marking is most usual, occasionally individual koi with black tancho markings

The simplicity of Tancho Kohaku is very demanding, in appreciation terms. White skin must be especially clear and unstained.

A very unusually shaped tancho marking.

The clean impression is quickly lost when white skin becomes stressed.

appear. These are called kuro tancho, and are clasfied as Kawarigoi, unless the koi is metallic based.

Evolution

The tancho marking, as a key feature of this variety, was originally desired to be large, round, solidly coloured, and to have clean sharp edges. The (ideally) round hi should cover as much of the head as possible, but without incursion over eyes or shoulders; hence the koi with a broad forehead would be more likely to develop the classic tancho. While this is still preferred, other shapes and sizes of tancho have become acceptable: for example the kakutan, or square tancho; or the umebachi, a shape like the petal of the Japanese apricot blossom.

In the final analysis, the overall balance of the impression is always the most important factor. Unusually shaped tancho markings may be extremely attractive in combination with other features, for example the arrangement of black (sumi) on Tancho Sanke and Showa.

Basic Principles of Tancho Appreciation

There is far more to a good tancho koi than just a well defined, round red marking on the head. However close to 'perfection' this individual feature may be, the rest of the koi must demonstrate the requisite criteria for high quality, in structured appreciation terms. Firstly, an excellent conformation – that is, a well shaped head, body and finnage, in proportion with each other. Secondly, clear, bright, lustrous skin with well balanced, solid, clear-edged body-pattern components (that is, when any are present, for instance the sumi of Sanke, Showa); and thirdly, a pleasing, alert deportment. All these additional factors must be taken into consideration, since appreciation is of the entire koi, never of a single feature in isolation.

Tancho Kohaku

The Tancho Kohaku is perhaps the epitome of the tancho ideal, a plain white background with the simplest of overlay, a single head hi: providing a picture of unsophisticated elegance, but stunning, when the koi is of a high quality.

With such a plain base, perfect symmetry of line, in both body shape and finnage, is an absolute requirement. Furthermore, such a large expanse of white skin is highly demanding of a smooth, lustrous, unblemished, pure white finish. Scaling must also be neat, since any unevenness of the scale lines (kokenami) is very obvious on a koi where the entire body is a single colour.

Because there are few individual elements present to appreciate, what there are must be to an exactingly high standard. Probably the most common problem seen on this type of koi at shows is a (usually) stress-related flushing of the white skin, which considerably damages the impression. Nevertheless, a Tancho Kohaku that merits the epithet 'excellent' is undoubtedly, a truly memorable koi.

Tancho Sanke

A Tancho Sanke may broadly be compared to a Shiro Bekko, a 'white-based' koi with black, but demonstrating an additional head hi. No hi must appear on the body of the koi.

The quality and arrangement of sumi on the body is essentially that required for Sanke or Shiro Bekko. Traditionally, sumi markings have tended to be fairly small and numerous, rounded in appear-

ance, and confined to the back above the lateral line for these varieties, although in latter years much variation in shape, size, position and number of markings has appeared.

Ideally the sumi should be dense, blue-black and clear-bordered. The impression of 'floating' on the skin surface, originally ascribed to the appearance of Sanke-style sumi, has largely been supplanted in recent years by the development of sumi markings that give the feeling of greater depth, due to the demonstration of deep blue sashi at the leading edges. This effect has been more fully described in preceding chapters. Very small speckles of sumi (jari or gravel) are undesirable as they provoke an untidy and unfinished look. Sumi markings on a Tancho Sanke are of highest impact when relatively few in number, large enough to fit the koi, similar in size and evenly arranged along the back from an inital shoulder marking, to give a 'stepping stone' impression.

Below: *An unusual Tancho Sanke with an almost square tancho marking. Sumi on the body adds interest.*

Above: *Sumi on the head of a Tancho Showa quite often bisects the tancho marking.*

Although this very unusual Tancho Showa is attractive, the sumi is completely undeveloped. The tancho marking looks flower-like.

A very unusual koi, a Kage Tancho Showa. The kage scaling is unfortunately rather indistinct.

The highest quality sumi has a blue tone from Asagi Magoi lineage, providing the greatest depth of impression when demonstrating deep blue insertion under white scales at the leading edge of each sumi marking (sashi). No sumi is expected on the head of a Tancho Sanke.

Finnage

Finnage carrying a few light stripes (tejima or tezumi) is thought to indicate sumi of greater stability on the body of the koi, as well as providing elegance. Too many stripes give a heavy appearance to the koi. Plain white finnage is also quite acceptable for appreciation.

In summary: a Tancho Sanke with an excellent conformation, clear white skin, well defined, attractively balanced, dense sumi with the addition of a solid, large, bright tancho provides a very impressive image.

Tancho Showa

A Tancho Showa essentially has the tri-coloured head of a Showa combined with the black and white body of a Shiro Utsuri. Hi should appear on the head alone. Like all Showa and Utsurimono, sumi is expected on the head of a Tancho Showa, where it often bisects the tancho marking, providing great character and individualism. The appearance of the white skin should be the equal of that seen on modern Kohaku or Sanke; indeed, great improvements have been made to the basic quality of Showa over the last decade.

The sumi of Tancho Showa is quite different in character to that of Tancho Sanke: it is often far more asymmetrical, jagged and extensive, and wraps around the body below the lateral line, as has been previously discussed. Although modern (kindai) Tancho Showa have a much higher proportion of white skin than was traditionally seen, the actual arrangement, style and appearance of the sumi, together with the presence of fin joint (motoguro) and head sumi, are usually distinguishing features from Tancho Sanke.

Showa sumi should look intrinsic to the koi, as if emerging from within the skin, and giving the impression of great depth. The colour should be a solid and homogeneous ebony or bluish-black, with a shiny lacquered finish and sharp trailing edges (kiwa) to the pattern elements. No scaling should be visible through the sumi. Showa sumi patterns are highly variable, but in terms of appreciation are in fact only required to demonstrate balance.

Perhaps less powerful in impact than fully three-coloured Showa, a high quality Tancho Showa is a koi very difficult to achieve, therefore highly prized. The stark black and white of the body is unforgiving of defects. For example, the presence of any nabe (greyish) or unfinished sumi is far more unacceptable on a Tancho Showa than on a full Showa, where the grey may blend into red and white patterns to create a pleasing impression. In this respect, appreciation of Tancho Showa is more closely related to that of Shiro Utsuri. However, the combination of jagged ink black over pure white, together with the undeniably bold statement of a deeply coloured, large head hi on a superbly configured koi, probably affords this Tancho variety with the highest impact.

Kin-Gin-Rin Scaling

All three Tancho varieties that are classified in this group may demonstrate kin-gin-rin scaling (rows of brightly shining scales along the back and sides of the koi). On the very plain Tancho Kohaku such an overlay can be a considerable enhancement to the overall impression. However, opinions vary over the merit of kin-gin-rin appearing on any patterned koi (a topic that will be examined in detail in the chapter dedicated to kin-gin-rin koi). In the final analysis, any appreciation of the additional feature of kin-gin-rin scaling on Tancho Sanke or Showa must be made in consideration with other appreciation points demonstrated by a particular koi.

In Conclusion

Tancho koi are a group demonstrating an interesting pattern variation that is popular with many hobbyists. The impression they give can be quite variable, often light-hearted, always appealing. A tancho koi makes an interesting addition to any collection of koi.

7 Asagi/Shusui

Asagi / Shusui at a Glance

These are blue koi with a vignette or scale reticulation in a darker blue. Asagi are fully scaled (wagoi) and Shusui doitsu, (either kagamigoi, having rows of large scales along the dorsal and lateral lines only, or kawagoi, having almost no scales at all). Red (hi) patterns typically appear along the sides of the head and body and as red pectoral fin joints (motoaka). The names of Asagi / Shusui refer to colour variants.

Konjo Asagi	(very dark blue/purple base)
Narumi Asagi	(pale blue with a darker vignette. The best known Asagi)
Hi Asagi	(an Asagi where the hi around the sides of the koi has extended over the back)
Taki or waterfall Asagi	(a light blue, non-reticulated band of colour divides the typical Asagi, blue-reticulated dorsal area from a red abdomen)
Mizu or water Asagi	(a very pale blue/white Asagi)
Shusui	(a light blue koi with the doitsu scales reticulated as for Asagi. Hi appears around the sides of the head and body)
Hana Shusui	(hi markings like strings of beads appear between the dorsal and lateral scale lines)
Hi Shusui	(hi extends over the back of the koi)
Ki Shusui	(yellow patterns replace the hi)
Kosui	(crossbred koi between Kohaku and Shusui, red patterns are similiar to those of Kohaku, may also be classified with Kawarigoi)

Not Classified with Asagi / Shusui for Show Purposes

	Show Class
Ginsui or Kinsui (metallic Shusui)	Hikarimoyo
Sanke or Showa Shusui	Kawarigoi

Features

Kin-gin-rin scaling:	Rows of very shiny scales appearing on the back and sides of the koi (Asagi). Shusui may occasionally demonstrate pearl scales.

Introduction

Blue-based and with a very different style to other koi, Asagi are thought to be the very first recognized variety of nishikigoi, from records dating back about one hundred and fifty years. The doitsu version of the fully scaled Asagi is called Shusui, which means 'autumn water'. Shusui are characterized by lines of large scales that run along the dorsal and lateral lines only.

Evolution

Historically, Shusui were produced a few decades after the appearance of Asagi by crossbreeding those early blue koi that also demonstrated quite extensive hi (red) markings, with European mirror carp (kagamigoi). Mr Kichigoro Akiyama is credited with producing this first doitsu Shusui around 1911. A further variant, also known as doitsu, is the leather carp (kawagoi), with no scales, or very few. Since the scale lines of Shusui are an appreciation point, kawagoi tend to be rarely seen in this variety.

Identification and Appearance

The Asagi-Shusui blue base can be a variety of shades, from almost white (Mizu or water Asagi) to a very dark, purplish-blue (Konjo Asagi), close to the original Asagi Magoi in type. A basic feature of all these koi is the reticulated or vignette effect, produced as a result of each individual scale area having different shades of blue. The darker area usually occurs over the centre of each scale, shading to a paler blue, grey or, ideally, almost white border, in the Narumi Asagi style. The name was given due to the pattern's resemblance to a tie-dyed cloth called 'narumi-shibori'.

Occasionally Asagi or Shusui are seen with the dark portion of each scale area located at the edges, with a lighter centre. Konjo Asagi may be seen to demonstrate this arrangement. The extent and contrast of the darker area of scales, for both Konjo and Narumi styles, is quite variable between individual koi.

It is generally thought that, for excellence, both Asagi and Shusui must demonstrate some hi; this usually occurs on the cheeks, in the pectoral fins and along the sides of the koi, an arrangement peculiar to this variety. However, it must be remembered that the absence of hi on an Asagi or Shusui, where all other appreciation points are met at a very high level of quality, should not disqualify a koi. In the author's experience, several show-winning Asagi-Shusui have had either minimal or no hi markings. It is interesting to note that the so-called 'secondary hi' of Go-Sanke varieties (Kohaku, Sanke and Showa) appearing below the lateral line, is also known as 'Asagi hi' and points to the origins of these koi.

Both Asagi and Shusui change radically as they age, generally becoming lighter coloured. The amount of hi usually increases over the years, and may spread to cover almost the entire body in some cases.

Hana Shusui have a clear blue border separating hi from dorsal and lateral scale lines.

A neatly finished Asagi. The hi is strong, and the red rim to the dorsal fin gives a pleasing touch of colour.

The clean white head and well defined vignette of this Asagi more than outweigh the minimal hi.

An example of a Shusui with very extensive hi.

Asagi often develop more hi, spreading over the back, as they grow older.

Basic Principles for Asagi/Shusui Appreciation

The basic requirements for koi appreciation are a good conformation (the overall shape and proportion of body, head and finnage); high quality, lustrous skin; and an alert, interested deportment. These characteristics are as important for Asagi-Shusui as for any other, more modern variety. Specific appreciation points apply to both fully scaled Asagi and doitsu-scaled Shusui, but with varying emphasis. The heads of both should be spotlessly clean. Colour is usually white or pale blue, although the shade is of less importance than the impression of absolute clarity. Any red pigmentation on the head may be confined to a fine line around the nose and cheeks, or may extend as a wide band above the eyes, leaving only the forehead blue or white.

In recent years interest has focused on new hi pattern styles for Asagi and Shusui. For example, both are now being developed with forehead hi. Classically, the arrangement of hi centred along the sides of the head and body has been a particular appreciation point of this group, together with the very clear, unblemished blue or white forehead. From the cheeks, hi traditionally extends along the lateral line area and into the pectoral fins from a red joint (Motoaka). In the light of such developments, this appreciation point may require re-evaluation in future.

An Asagi showing fully red pectorals, or 'red hands'.

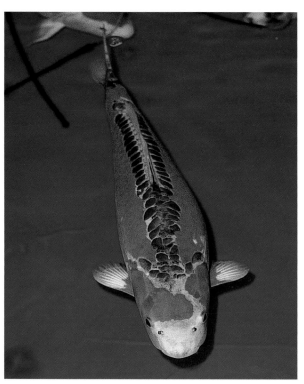

Right: *A Hi Shusui showing the problem of uneven scaling.*

A Hi Shusui of excellent quality.

Hi Colour and Pattern

The colour of hi should be fiery red and very bright. Its quality is quite different to that of Kohaku, Sanke or Showa, appearing more intrinsic to the skin than a thick overlay of colour. Scaling, when present, is usually quite easily visible. The origin of hi is the red belly of the Asagi Magoi. Hi may also be visible in the tail and at the base of the dorsal fin, as well as in the pectoral fins. If the pectoral fins, or 'hands', are completely red, they are highly regarded.

Shusui that have a narrow strip of hi between the dorsal and lateral scale lines are called Hana (flowery) Shusui. If hi extends over the back, as it often does in older examples, the koi is called Hi Asagi or Shusui. Occasionally hi takes over completely, with no background blue colour remaining visible: such a koi would be reclassified as Aka Matsuba in Kawarigoi, a red koi with a purple/black vignette.

The Vignette

The quality of the vignette is another, all-important appreciation point for the Asagi-Shusui group. It is particularly obvious on the fully scaled classic (Narumi) Asagi, since there is no other pattern over the light blue back to distract the eye. Each scale area should look precisely defined, as a dark triangular wedge with a paler surrounding lattice; the greater the contrast between the shades of blue involved, the more powerful is the impression given by the vignette.

A common fault is the blurred, out-of-focus finish shown by many Asagi, due to lack of definition

A rare and beautiful Kin-Gin-Rin Asagi.

of the vignette coupled with colours rather more grey than blue. This appearance is often typical of young Asagi, up to three years old, since the clarity of the vignette may be slow to develop. Many Asagi in the UK unfortunately also produce small sumi spots all over the head and body as they age, which detracts from the clean impression so important for this variety. The question of causative agent for this problem has never really been resolved, although many people believe that water quality plays an important role. Shusui are affected more severely, often turning almost completely black.

Scaling

Uniformity of scale size and placement is a feature particularly vital to the doitsu Shusui, although even scaling is also important for Asagi. Lines of scales should be neat and highly symmetrical; odd 'redundant' scales (mudagoke) give an untidy impression. Asagi-Shusui is one of the few koi varieties where symmetry of pattern and scaling are of particular importance as appreciation points.

An unusual Asagi, with a maruten head hi and kanoko (dappled) hi along the flanks.

Occasionally, very unusual Asagi-Shusui appear. Hi on Asagi can occur as Kanoko (dappled), each scale area having a red centre. Kin-Gin-Rin Asagi-Shusui are uncommon, but make interesting variants. Silver-edged, dark-centred scales on the Shusui make a pleasing contrast (Platinum Shusui). The Taki (waterfall) Asagi has an interesting light blue, non-reticulated band along each flank between a darker, lightly reticulated back and red belly.

Crossbred Asagi-Shusui

Asagi-Shusui have been crossbred with many other varieties over the years to produce some very distinctive koi. Examples are:

- **Metallic Kin or Ginsui:** a silver-blue doitsu koi with darker reticulated scale areas and orange/gold Asagi-Shusui hi, now rarely seen.
- **Sanke-Shusui cross:** a blue-based doitsu koi showing Sanke hi and sumi, as well as Asagi-Shusui hi and a vignette over the blue scales.
- **Showa-Shusui cross:** typical Showa markings on a Shusui base.
- **Ai-Goromo:** a white and red koi with a blue vignette over the hi. A cross between Asagi and Kohaku.
- **Goshiki:** a basic red and white koi with shades of blue and black as an overlaying scale reticulated effect on white skin only (modern Goshiki), or as a vignette on both hi and white (traditional Goshiki). The most common cross for Goshiki is between Asagi and Taisho Sanke.
- **Kosui:** a Shusui crossed with Kohaku, resulting in a (usually) very pale blue, or almost white base, darker, reticulated blue scales and hi appearing in patterns similar to those of Kohaku, very different from traditional Shusui.

In Conclusion

Asagi-Shusui are beautiful koi and worthy of any collection. The contrast of bright hi and clearly defined light and dark blue colours can be quite breathtaking, especially on a large koi. The impression is of clear, rippled water. It would be very pleasing to see more of this variety in the future; these graceful koi, of ancient lineage, should take a more well deserved and prominent place in our ponds.

8 Koromo

Koromo at a Glance

Koromo are a group of koi patterned similarly to Kohaku, Sanke and Showa, with the additional common feature of a vignette or scale reticulations over the red patterns (hi) or, in the case of Goshiki, over white and red, or over white only. The vignette may be blue or black in colour.

Ai-Goromo	(Koromo with a blue vignette over hi on the body only)
Sumi Goromo	(Koromo with a black vignette over all hi elements)
Budo Goromo (Sanke)	(Koromo with purple, grape-like markings over small groups of scales)
Koromo Sanke	(a Sanke with Koromo scale reticulation overlaying the hi)
Koromo Showa	(a Showa with Koromo scale reticulation overlaying the hi)
Goshiki Sanke	(a Sanke with Koromo scale reticulation overlaying hi and white)
Goshiki Showa	(a Showa with Koromo scale reticulation overlaying hi and white)
Goshiki	(a group demonstrating much variability as to proportions of basic red, white and black skin. A vignette that extends over the white skin is common to all, however, and traditional Goshiki also have the vignette effect over red skin, as well as being much darker in general appearance)
Tancho Goshiki	(a koi with blue or black reticulated skin, having a single hi marking, only on the head)
Kin-Gin-Rin Goshiki	(rows of very shiny scales appearing on the back and sides of the koi)

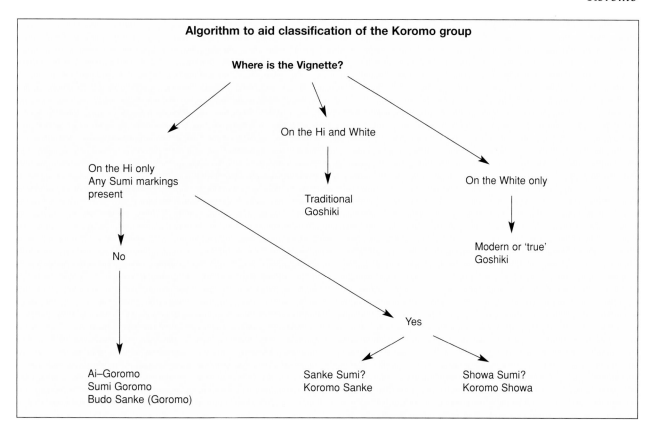

Algorithm to aid classification of the Koromo group

Where is the Vignette?

On the Hi only
Any Sumi markings
present

On the Hi and White

On the White only

↓

↓

↓

No

Traditional
Goshiki

Modern or 'true'
Goshiki

Yes

↓

Ai–Goromo
Sumi Goromo
Budo Sanke (Goromo)

Sanke Sumi?
Koromo Sanke

Showa Sumi?
Koromo Showa

Not Classified as Koromo for Show Purposes

	Show Class
Shochikubai (metallic Ai-Goromo)	Hikarimoyo
Metallic Goshiki equivalent	Hikarimoyo

Features

Doitsu	Either kagamigoi, having rows of large scales along the dorsal and lateral lines only; or kawagoi having almost no scales at all.
Menkaburi	The head of the koi is completely red.
Bozu	No hi appears on the head.
Specific hi patterns	Named as for Kohaku: nidan, sandan, inazuma, maruten.

Above: *Well defined, dark blue reticulations on a solid red base contrast strongly with clear white skin on a classic Ai-Goromo.*

Introduction

Koromo are multi-patterned, non-metallic koi with the additional feature of a vignette, or scale reticulation. All Koromo have a common Asagi bloodline (a blue koi with a well developed vignette) that is crossed with Kohaku (white with red patterns), Sanke ('white-based' with red and black patterns) and Showa ('black-based' with red and white patterns, different in character to Sanke) to produce the specific members of the group. They are most easily distinguished by simply referring to the position of the vignette with reference to the other pattern features.

Also classified with Koromo are doitsu (either kagamigoi, having rows of large scales along the dorsal and lateral lines only; or kawagoi, having almost no scales at all) and kin-gin-rin (rows of brilliantly shining scales along the back) Koromo.

Scale reticulation – also called 'amine', 'mesh in a net' or 'vignette' – is an important Koromo feature, and is common to several varieties of koi. It may appear in a range of strengths, from a faint lattice of colour around the scale edges, either darker than the centre, as in Chagoi, Ochiba Shigure, Sorogoi, classified as Kawarigoi, or paler, as many Ogon, classified as Hikarimuji; or as the very bold two-tone 'pine-cone effect' scales common to Asagi / Shusui and Matsubagoi. Regardless of the level of contrast of the colours over each scale area, consistency and clarity of the vignette along the body is a vital appreciation point for koi that demonstrate this feature.

A rare Goshiki Sanke.

The Koromo Vignette

Koromo means 'robed' or 'veiled', and refers to the commonest appearance of the vignette on these koi. The outer third of the area covering each scale tends to carry the darker colour, beginning from an indistinct melding of the colours towards the centre of each scale area, and finishing at the scale-edge point as a neat dark blue or black line. It is as though a wash of dark paint has been drawn gently across part of each scale area within hi elements, but has not completely covered them. Modern or 'true' Goshiki, having the vignette only over white scale areas, often show a characteristic wedge-shaped or pine-cone definition to their scale reticulation. Very reminiscent of their Asagi forebears, this style of vignette is much sharper and cleaner-looking than conventional Koromo robing.

Appreciating Koromo means remembering that it is a crossbred group, although characteristics from each parent are not equally expressed genetically. For example, Goshiki demonstrate very little or no honzumi (Sanke sumi, from the Sanke parent), only koromozumi. Certain attributes, however, of the original parent varieties are important appreciation points. A useful example is given by perhaps the best known Koromo, the Ai-Goromo. Kohaku was origi-

This Ai-Goromo demonstrates excellent Koromo 'robing'.

Note the reticulation appearing on the white skin of this Sumi Goromo. Sometimes referred to as 'going Goshiki'.

nally crossed with Asagi to produce this type of koi, where the robing over white skin, a Goshiki feature, has been completely eliminated. Specific appreciation points for Ai-Goromo, as well as other members of the Koromo group, rely on aspects from both Asagi and Kohaku lines.

Basic Principles of Koromo Appreciation

The first appreciation points to be looked for are those common to all varieties, and thus vital to remember. The overall shape or conformation of head, body and finnage must be strong and well proportioned, with excellent skin quality, soft, bright, lustrous and smooth-looking. The koi should look alert and balanced, with well displayed finnage.

Briefly (since details are available in an earlier chapter), Kohaku appreciation points are pure, unblemished white skin on which red (hi) patterns are superimposed in a balanced, pleasing manner with sharp, clear trailing edges to each coloured area (hiban). Interestingly, a stepped hi pattern is thought to be particularly desirable for Koromo. Hi should be present on the head, but should not be too predominant; it should appear thick, almost painted on. Homogeneity of colour along the head and body is desirable, although a deeper shading on the head may be expected due to the lack of scales in this area. Finnage should be clear white, unstained by hi, although red pectoral fin joints (motoaka) are acceptable, if they enhance the general pattern.

Koromo may take many years to develop. This young Ai-Goromo has only a minimal, delicate blue vignette.

More extensive robing can be seen on this Ai-Goromo.

A rarely seen Koromo koi. The Koromo Showa has reticulated hi on a Showa base.

A doitsu Koromo Sanke.

A Sumi Goromo showing the more typical, blurred reticulated effect.

Sumi Goromo can present a clean finish.

As discussed in the previous chapter, Asagi are usually a shade of pale blue (Narumi Asagi) with a darker vignette, but may vary from almost white (Mizu or water Asagi) to quite a dark blue (Konjo Asagi). Important points relevant to Koromo are a clear, unstained head, no sumi speckles on the body, and scale reticulation that looks precision-etched over each scale area, giving a high definition appearance. It is this particular characteristic, inherited by Koromo koi, that has the greatest significance. In fact, when examining many Koromo koi, the vignette is the only obvious feature from the Asagi parent.

Ai-Goromo

Young Ai-Goromo may be indistinguishable from Kohaku, since the blue scale reticulation on the hi may not develop until the koi is a few years old. Ai-Goromo are very elegant, having clear white skin and hi markings delicately etched with a blue vignette. The clear blue rim overlaying the area of each scale edge, particularly where the scale edges form the trailing edge of each hi element (maruzome or scalloped kiwa), enhances the clarity and definition of the kiwa. The bluish tinge created by the robing within each hiban tends to make the white skin look even whiter, in contrast.

Appreciation points for quality and placement of hi and white skin on Ai-Goromo are effectively the same as for Kohaku, with the additional requirement for a clear vignette – although due to the nature of the Koromo 'robing', definition is never as precise as that of Asagi /Shusui or Matsubagoi. It is important to remember that Ai-Goromo have blue scale reticulation confined to the hi markings on the body only. The head hi should be a clear, unstained red.

A little blue-tinted sashi is quite acceptable, where

the scales insert into the skin at the leading edge of each hiban, but kiwa should always be clearly defined. Thus, blue colour should not 'run' from the hi into white skin following the trailing edge of a pattern element. When this occurs, as it sometimes does for older Koromo, the koi is said to be 'going Goshiki', since it is the Goshiki variety which is typified by a reticulated effect over white skin. However, the contrast of pure white skin and neat, blue-reticulated hi, as demonstrated by a good example of an Ai-Goromo, is particularly striking. High quality Ai-Goromo are very attractive and unfortunately, quite rare koi.

Sumi Goromo

Sumi Goromo are Koromo where the reticulated effect, or robing, over hi elements is black (sumi) rather than blue. Their appearance is quite different from that of Ai-Goromo. The sumi has a more 'brushed-on' look, and overlays the head hi as well as hi on the body of the koi – in fact the reticulated effect is often very blurred for Sumi Goromo, and if too heavy, can make the koi look rather gloomy and dull-coloured. The clean-cut finish of any reticulated variety is most important to the overall impression the koi gives.

In recent years more attention has been given to the breeding of Sumi Goromo, and some quite spectacular examples are starting to be seen, with brilliantly clear, incredibly white skin offset by magnificent, almost purple markings, demonstrating a much cleaner, very dark vignette.

Budo-Sanke or Budo-Gormo

Budo-Sanke, or Budo Goromo, are rare Koromo offspring originally attributed to an Asagi / Kohaku cross that developed with dark purple markings covering small groups of scales, creating shapes like bunches of grapes, analogous to rare Gotenzakura koi found in pure Kohaku spawnings. Today, all Koromo demonstrating this very deep purple colour over hi, regardless of size of pattern elements, are known as Budo Goromo. As for other types of Koromo, pure white skin with balanced, well defined and strongly coloured markings are desirable features. In the author's experience, Budo Sanke are unusual in that the heads of these koi tend to carry very little pattern. However, a clean white head with the unusual, deep purple markings on the body provides an eye-catching contrast.

Koromo-Sanke and Koromo-Showa

These are koi resulting from various Koromo breeding programmes which at first glance appear to be Sanke or Showa. However, closer inspection reveals the presence of scale reticulation overlaying hi elements: this should appear well defined and neat.

Two excellent examples of modern Goshiki.

The changing faces of Goshiki.

In all other respects these koi should be appreciated on the points important to the basic Sanke and Showa varieties, detailed in earlier chapters. These koi are quite uncommon, and good examples rarely seen.

Goshiki

Goshiki are a fascinating group, placed in the Koromo show class in the UK because of the obvious similarities of appearance and lineage. Previously these koi were classified as Kawarigoi. In Japan and some other large Zen Nippon Airinkai (ZNA) shows, Goshiki may be classified separately.

It is reported that Goshiki were first produced around the turn of the century from Asagi crossed with Aka Bekko (a red koi with black patterns) or Aka Sanke (a Sanke with very extensive red patterns covering most of the head and body of the koi). In more recent years, Goshiki have been produced from Asagi crossed with Taisho Sanke. It has also been reported that introduction of Karasugoi bloodlines into Goshiki breeding programmes has had great impact upon their appearance.

Goshiki are said to be five-coloured – white, red, black, blue and purple – although to be able to distinguish all five colours on a single koi is not usually possible. The hi forms the most obvious and clearly defined pattern on most Goshiki, a desirable feature of which is thought to be a stepped layout along the back of the koi (i.e. nidan, sandan, yondan or godan). One problem that is often seen on Goshiki is an all-red head (menkaburi); head patterns as prescribed for Kohaku are preferred.

Scale reticulation in the traditional style extends over both hi and white skin. Originally, Goshiki often showed drab, very indistinct colours with an almost unrecognizable vignette. This was slowly improved, resulting in koi that were very eye-catching because of their particularly bright hi; unfortunately the rest of the body and head tended to be a very dark, poorly defined grey and black. Latterly, however, a tremendous improvement has been seen, and 'modern ' or 'true' Goshiki are now being produced that have extensive, brilliant white skin, bright, homogeneous hi, a vignette of high definition, and fascinating patterns.

On this type of Goshiki, the scale reticulation effect often resembles that of the Asagi more closely, in that the centres rather than the borders of the scale areas may be dark. The netting pattern often covers the white skin only, which provides a very clean and elegant finish as well as creating a dramatic three-dimensional effect with solid, non-reticulated hi elements. Another dramatic modern Goshiki is

A stunning Goshiki in a very individual style.

a variant where reticulated white skin is almost entirely replaced by lustrous looking black, over which, briliant hi appears to float. These Goshiki tend to demonstrate motoguro, suggesting the Karasugoi influence. Interest in this unusual group of koi has revived dramatically with the appearance of these often stunning examples.

In Conclusion

Koromo have perhaps been undervalued in the past. As a group they combine both elegance and high impact; they are also highly individual with great potential for excellence. For many years the Go-Sanke varieties – Kohaku, Sanke and Showa – have dominated the hobby, as they continue to do today; hence the improvement of other, less high profile varieties – for example Goshiki, Karasugoi, Ochiba Shigure – has been consequently slow, due principally to lack of demand. Perhaps in the future we will see more of these high quality, but less well recognized koi, as hobbyists begin to realize just what sort of high standard really superb examples can achieve.

9 Kin-Gin-Rin

Kin-Gin-Rin at a Glance

Koi with sparkling gold ('kin', over red or yellow) and/or silver ('gin', over white or black) scales may appear in any variety. If the koi is to merit classification as a kin-gin-rin the shiny scales should visibly comprise at least two, and preferably three (or more) complete rows on either side of the dorsal fin along the back. For show purposes, only Kohaku, Sanke, Showa and Shiro Utsuri are classified as the variety Kin-Gin-Rin. This group comprises the ZNA 'A', or 'Group 1' Kin-Gin-Rin class; ZNA 'B', or 'Group 2' Kin-Gin-Rin comprise all other kin-gin-rin koi.

Kin-Gin-Rin Kohaku
Kin-Gin-Rin Sanke
Kin-Gin-Rin Showa

Not Classified as Kin-Gin-Rin (A) for Show Purposes

All other kin-gin-rin koi other than those listed above – for example, Gin-Rin Shiro Bekko – would be in Bekko (UK) or 'B' Kin-Gin-Rin (ZNA).Koi with Type 3 scaling would be as detailed below.

Features

Kin-Gin-Rin scales:

Type 1: Pearl	The scales have a lumpy, three-dimensional shiny deposit in the centre of each scale.
Type 2: Flat	The shine looks two-dimensional, either appearing as lines across the scales (cracked glass), the so-called diamond

or Hiroshima kin-gin-rin; or as beta-gin, where the whole scale shines equally.

Type 3: Rim

Occasionally koi appear with a very delicate, shiny edge to each scale, only a few millimetres across. This has been confused with fukurin, since a faint lattice finish is achieved. Such koi are not classified with Kin-Gin-Rin.

A Matsunosuke Sanke showing only partially shiny scales.

Introduction

Kin-gin-rin refers to koi that possess rows of mirror-like, brightly shining scales; ideally these rows will be unbroken and should be most visible along the back. The prefix 'kin' means gold, and 'gin' silver.

"Kin and gin" refer to the background colour of the koi on which the scales appear. For instance, if the shining scales are associated with white or black skin, they appear silver: thus a Shiro Bekko (a 'white-based' koi with black patterns) with bright scales would be a Gin-Rin Shiro Bekko, and a yellow or red-skinned koi (Kigoi–yellow, or Benigoi–red) would be called kin-rin, when the shiny scales are present.

Koi such as Kohaku (a white koi with red patterns) or Goshiki (a basic red and white koi with shades of blue and/or black as an overlaying scale reticulated effect, or vignette) tend to have both kin-rin and gin-rin scales. It is quite rare for the shining scales to be confined to a single colour on a multi-patterned koi, since a usual and desirable feature of kin-gin-rin koi is that the shining scales should be visible along the entire length of the back.

For a koi to be classified as a kin-gin-rin, the shining scales must appear as at least two, and preferably three (or more) rows on either side of the dorsal fin. Technically, they should also be bright enough to appear obvious when the koi is viewed from any direction. Many koi have just a few, scattered shiny scales.

In recent years, considerable confusion has occurred over some Go-Sanke (Kohaku, Sanke and Showa). Koi of these varieties occasionally demonstrate either a few rows of partially shiny scales (usually the outer third of each scale), often along the lateral lines, or a more subtle shine, particularly visible on scales within white pattern elements, said to be a feature of the Matsunosuke bloodline. It has been speculated that this so-called 'Matsunosuke shine' is a rudimentary form of Hiroshima gin rin. More importantly, koi demonstrating this shine have also been said to

Above: *This elegant young Sanke presents a problem: should it be classified as Kin-Gin-Rin? Shiny scales show only over white skin.*

Above right: *A Kin-Gin-Rin Kohaku.*

be displaying fukurin, which is misleading, since the term fukurin does not refer to 'shine on scales'.

Fukurin

Broadly this means a reticulated appearance, arising from the interaction of skin and scales with light; it is said to appear as two forms, depending upon how many layers create the reticulated effect; these layers are formed from middle and upper skin. This layering effect of skin and scales, the subtle or dramatic difference in pigmentation between the layers, and the difference in light reflection by scales and surrounding skin, all combine to produce the netting effect most commonly associated with Ogon (from both Hikarimuji and Hikarimoyo), Asagi and Matsuba varieties. These classes of koi are reported to demonstrate fukurin created by just one layer of (originally) middle skin growing over the scales. The second type of fukurin, involving multiple layers of skin, is said to be quite rare.

On koi not typically associated with having a netting pattern to the skin, such as the Go-Sanke varieties, fukurin is a subtle and easily missed point of appreciation. The effect is most likely to be visible over the white skin only, on adult and mature koi. Interestingly, it has recently been reported that efforts are being made to reduce scale size genetically on some of the Go-Sanke lines, in order to better demonstrate fukurin; however, the author cannot confirm this at the time of writing.

Evolution

To return to true kin-gin-rin koi, they are accredited with quite a long history. It is widely reported that they were first discovered and named by Mr Eizaburo Hoshino, a great contributor to the improvement of Nishikigoi, in 1929. There are several variations in type of kin-gin-rin scales; perhaps the most commonly seen is diamond gin that gives a 'cracked glass' appearance, each scale having brightly shining lines running across it from the insertion point to the edge. This type of kin-gin-rin has also been known as Hiroshima gin, since it was first noticed on a koi from this area in 1969.

Beta gin scales are completely shiny and display a flat brilliance; this type of kin-gin-rin is the most rare, and also considered to be the most refined. Pearl kin-gin-rin provides a more three-dimensional shine; rarely seen, pearl scales have a bright 'lump' in the centre of each scale.

With the exception of pearl kin-gin-rin, it is important that the whole width of each kin-gin-rin scale is shiny; on some koi only the outer half or third of the scale shows the kin-gin-rin effect.

Basic Principles of Kin-Gin-Rin Appreciation

Kin-gin-rin may be regarded as an 'add-on' feature in appreciation terms, and the excellence of the basic koi variety must never be forgotten. For example, spectacular kin-gin-rin on a koi with a poor conformation (overall shape and proportions of head, body and finnage), or with yellow-tinged and/or coarse-grained white skin, will never be able to achieve true impressiveness. Think instead about the impression of the same quality kin-gin-rin appearing on a koi having many of the desirable, basic quality elements. To reiterate, these include an excellent conformation;

This Ogon clearly demonstrates the net effect known as fukurin.

A Gin-Rin Shiro Utsuri (no hi, therefore no kin scales).

This Sanke has strong hi and well defined sumi. The hi pattern is unusual, and the kin-gin-rin scaling is strong. Only the rather yellow head detracts from the impression.

A Gin-Rin Ochiba Shigure (classified as Kawarigoi in the absence of a 'B' Kin-Gin-Rin class).

A neatly patterned Godan (five-step) Kin-Gin-Rin Kohaku.

Delicate kin-gin-rin scaling enhances the rather light hi on this Showa, without affecting the attractive, dense sumi.

83

A good quality Kin-Gin-Rin Kohaku.

smooth, lustrous, fine-grained skin; glowing, solid, well coloured, sharp-edged pattern elements; coupled with an alert deportment. The excellence of the kin-gin-rin scaling must always be viewed in balance with all the other appreciation points, including those important to particular varieties: for example, the definition of the vignette, or scale reticulation on Goshiki; or clear, 'speckle-free' white, yellow or red skin on Utsurimono ('black-based' koi with one other colour, this being white, red or yellow).

Classification of Kin-Gin-Rin

Theoretically, any koi variety may produce kin-gin-rin scales, although for show purposes only Kohaku, Sanke, and Showa are included in the show class Kin-Gin-Rin. All other kin-gin-rin koi are classified with their basic varieties. Zen Nippon Airinkai (ZNA) show classification includes a second kin-gin-rin class, "B", or "Group 2" Kin-Gin-Rin, which contains all these other kin-gin-rin koi.

In recent years, kin-gin-rin scaling seems to be gaining in popularity and appearing on a wider range of varieties. Many single-coloured koi, metallic and non metallic (Hikarimuji, Chagoi, Kigoi, and Sorogoi), take on a new dimension of impressiveness when

overlaid by kin-gin-rin scales. It is important to be aware of a basic appreciation point for metallic koi, however, when viewing kin-gin-rin variants: that is, the lustre or flat brilliance demonstrated by the skin is vital. When kin-gin-rin scales are present, their brightness may mask an underlying lack of lustre. High lustre, clearly visible on the head and pectorals of a metallic kin-gin-rin scaled koi, points to high quality skin.

Kin-Gin-Rin Controversy

There has been much controversy over the years about kin-gin-rin. Does it enhance the beauty of the koi or detract from it? There is no doubt that the shiny scales are eye-catching, although some hobbyists regard them as too 'flashy'. However, several problems affecting other appreciation points ensue. For instance, pattern edges that need to be sharp, can look blurred by the kin-gin-rin. Depth and homogeneity of red (hi) may be difficult to assess with a gold overlay. Black (sumi) skin may appear grey due to the reflective quality of the kin-gin-rin.

In recent years, however, improving standards of quality across most koi varieties has meant that kin-gin-rin has also benefited. For instance, much crisper pattern elements are being preserved, despite the shiny overlay; also the brightness of the kin-gin-rin scales, as well as their even distribution from head to tail – vital appreciation points – are improving. Some koi appear quite mirror-like.

In Conclusion

In the final analysis, the appreciation of kin-gin-rin can be a very personal and subjective point. It would seem, by their increased popularity alone, that some varieties have benefited quite dramatically from the introduction of kin-gin-rin scaling. Single-coloured Kawarigoi (Chagoi, Sorogoi, Kigoi, Benigoi) take on a very attractive, bright new 'look' with kin-gin-rin scaling, and are now appearing regularly at shows. These koi, previously not well represented on the showground, have been described as having 'a quiet elegance' – although this might be interpreted as not being highly visible!

It is perhaps more difficult to assess the benefit of kin-gin-rin on a koi with many original pattern elements already in place, where the addition of kin-gin-rin may offend the eye by the effect of over-patterning. However, it is undeniable that some spectacular multi-patterned kin-gin-rin koi are now being seen. As always, it is the balance of the entire koi that makes or breaks the final impression. When kin-gin-rin scales are uniformly bright and evenly distributed, without detriment to edges or colour of pattern elements, on a koi meeting other appreciation criteria to a high standard, then it would be difficult to deny the beauty of this variety.

10 Kawarigoi

Kawarigoi at a Glance

Kawarigoi is a very large group, and as such it is easier to examine them as four sections.

Group 1: Karasugoi

The Karasugoi may still be thought of as basically black. Most of the members of this group have very extensive sumi. Fully scaled varieties are named according to the positioning of white skin, whereas all doitsu Karasugoi with white patterns on the head and/or body are called Kumonryu. The distribution of black and white on the Karasu group is quite distinctive when compared to Shiro Utsuri. Generally, patterns appear to stream from head to tail, rather than to cross the back.

Hajiro	(a black, fully scaled koi with white tail and pectoral fin tips)
Hagashiro	(as for Hajiro, with additional white on the head)
Yotsushiro	(as for Hajiro and Hagashiro, with additional white on the dorsal and caudal fins)
Suminagashi	(a black, fully scaled koi with scales reticulated in white)
Matsukawabake	(a black and white patterned, fully scaled koi where the black and white areas reverse over time, or even seasonally)
Kumonryu	(a black and white patterned doitsu koi)
Beni Kumonryu	(a Kumonryu where the white patterns are largely replaced by red)

Group 2: Single-Coloured Koi

This group may or may not demonstrate scale reticulation, or fukurin, with a deeper shade of the base colour or with black. Fully reticulated koi have a very distinctive vignette and are called the Matsubagoi: for example Aka Matsuba, a red koi with a vignette pattern.

Kawarigoi

Matsubagoi (reticulated)

Aka Matsuba	(red)
Ki Matsuba	(yellow)
Shiro Matsuba	(white)

Non-Reticulated

Shiromuji	(a white koi)
Kigoi	(a yellow koi)
Benigoi	(a deep red koi; it occasionally has white fin tips)
Midorigoi	(a green or greenish-yellow koi)
Murasakigoi	(a lavender-coloured koi)
Sorogoi	(a pale grey koi; it may have a delicate vignette)
Chagoi	(a brown koi. Many shades of brown exist, from fawn to chocolate. A delicate vignette may be seen)

A Karasu, or 'Crow koi'.

Group 3: Crossbred Koi

The parent varieties are usually identifiable from the pattern and scaling of these koi. Names often simply indicate the cross, for example Sanke-Shusui, a koi with the basic red, white and black Sanke patterning, but also showing the blue background colour of Shusui. The best known in this group is the Ochiba Shigure ('autumn leaves on water'), variously reported to be a natural variant of Chagoi breeding programmes, the result of a cross between Chagoi and Sorogoi, or Chagoi and Ogon – or, more recently, between Chagoi and Kohaku.

Ochiba Shigure	(orange/brown and grey patterns)
Sanke-Shusui	(Sanke/Shusui cross)
Showa-Shusui	(Showa/Shusui cross)
Utsuri-Chagoi	(Utsurimono/Chagoi cross)
Kosui	(Kohaku/Shusui cross)

Group 4: 'Oddities'

These are rare koi that appear in any non-metallic variety, and are too unusual to compare with other koi in that variety. For example, Kanoko (dappled fawn) koi appearing in Kohaku, Sanke or Showa have hi which appears as a delicate reticulated scale pattern, rather than the solid areas of colour that would normally be seen.

Kanoko Kohaku	
Kanoko Sanke	
Kanoko Showa	
Gotenzakura	(a Kohaku with areas of hi which involves very small groups of scales, giving a bunch of grapes appearance
Kinzakura	(as for Gotenzakura, with gold borders to the hi elements)
Kage Utsuri	(Utsurimono, Shiro, Hi or Ki with shadowed white skin)

Not Classified with Kawarigoi for Show Purposes

In Japan at the time of writing the metallic Ki Kokuryu and Kin Ki Kokuryu (metallic Kumonryu and Beni Kumonryu equivalents respectively) are classified with Kawarigoi. In the UK they are placed with Hikarimoyo as a crossbred group, even though they are technically 'black-based' koi.

	Show Class
Goshiki	Koromo, UK. Goshiki may be given its own class at large ZNA shows.
Kage Showa	Showa, UK only.
Kanoko Asagi	Asagi / Shusui.

Introduction

The word 'kawari' means something strange or with peculiar characteristics. The Kawarigoi group is thus often perceived as a 'catch-all' for non-metallic koi that do not fit into the other show categories, and it therefore includes some that are very unusual. Although the epithet 'unique' is often used to describe members of this group, the word is misleading since every koi with a pattern is unique in the sense that no two patterns are ever identical. Kawarigoi comprise a group that inexperienced koi hobbyists find most difficult to classify: I find it is best to think of them as being members of four sub-groups with quite distinct features, for the most part; these are:

- The Karasugoi.
- Single-coloured koi, with and without a full vignette or fukurin
- Crossbred koi
- 'Oddities'

The popularity of Kawarigoi has increased in the UK in the last few years; they appear much more regularly on the showground, and some very high quality examples are being seen. However, it is important to remember that just because a koi looks very unusual, it is not automatically of high quality. Any koi, whatever its classification, has the same basic requirements for excellence, be it a Suminagashi or a Sanke: these are good conformation (meaning the overall shape and the proportions of the head, body and finnage); smooth, bright, lustrous skin; and an alert deportment. This is vital when appreciating such individual koi as are found in Kawarigoi. Let us now examine each of the sub-groups in turn.

The Karasugoi

Karasu means 'crow', and refers to the coal-black basic colour of these koi, thought to originate from the Asagi Magoi line through a Konjo Asagi (a dark blue, fully scaled koi with a darker reticulated pattern to each scale area). A brief look at the classification of the Karasugoi group shows us that Karasu variations are principally named according to the position and extent of the white skin when the koi is fully scaled. Thus the **Hajiro** has just white tail and pectoral fin tips, the **Hagashiro** is like a Hajiro but with white on the head, while the **Yotsushiro** is like a Hageshiro with additional white on the dorsal and caudal fins. **Suminagashi**, a rare and elegant koi, is required to show well developed and clear scale reticulation (vignette), meaning that each scale should display a well defined black and white area.

A Matsukawabake, darker at the tail end and around the nose.

A Matsukawabake: note the reverse arrangement of dark and light areas.

A Hageshiro.

This koi demonstrates the position of white skin as it would appear on a Hajiro. However, since it is a doitsu koi, despite the minimal white, it is called a Komonryu.

A Suminagashi, demonstrating a full black and white vignette pattern.

A young Beni Kumonryu.

A Beni Kumonryu with additional white skin.
'Incomplete' Beni Kumonryu are common.

The changing faces of Kumonryu.

Kawarigoi

Matsukawabake

These are fully scaled Karasugoi that demonstrate changing black and white patterns over time; they appear to develop an increasing proportion of white skin with age. When they are young they may resemble Hagashiro or Yotsushiro quite closely, with an additional white area over the shoulder. When white skin predominates – this may be in the summer months – this type of koi is usually recognizable by the position of the black skin (sumi), which tends to wrap around the nose and cheeks on the head, along the lateral lines, and spreads over the back behind the dorsal fin. In addition, narrow bands of sumi often outline the gill plates. There is a similarity to the positioning of red (hi) on many Asagi/Shusui. Recently, kin-gin-rin scaling (rows of very shiny scales along the back and sides) has begun to appear on Matsukawabake; when this is of good quality, it adds considerable emphasis to these already highly distinctive koi.

Kumonryu

These koi are always doitsu (with rows of large scales running only along dorsal and lateral lines, kagamigoi; if they have no scales at all, kawagoi). The pattern for Kumonryu was originally named after Japanese dragon paintings it was thought to resemble, because of the wavy lines of white on black, appearing along the flanks of the koi between the rows of scales. The position of this most eye-catching pattern is identical to that of hi on a Hana Shusui, described in a previous chapter. Latterly, any doitsu Karasugoi with white on the body and/or head is called a Kumonryu.

Breeders of this now exceptionally popular variety have overcome many early problems: for example, failure of these koi to grow beyond 50 or 60cm (20 to 24in), and extreme instability of the patterning, similar to that of Matsukawabake, from which line Kumonryu are said to originate. Contemporary Kumonryu are much more stable in their appearance over time, and may attain over 80cm (32in) in length, although they are still highly susceptible to changes in their environment.

Beni Kumonryu

A relatively new addition to this group, the beni Kumonryu is essentially a black doitsu Karasugoi with red (hi) patterns instead of white, although it may demonstrate some white skin in addition to hi. As yet this variety of Kumonryu is relatively rare. No large examples (over 40cm(16in)) have been seen by the author. It is possible that the hi has not yet been stabilized.

It is difficult to understand why, under ZNA rules the metallic Kumonryu equivalents (Ki Kokuryu and Kin Ki Kokuryu) are classified with Kawarigoi, a non-metallic group. In this book they are described with Hikarimoyo.

In Summary

The Karasugoi are particularly striking, and present a powerful image with their stark black and white beauty. Good examples should have deep, velvety, lustrous, bluish-black sumi that appears even in texture; no scales should be visible through it. White skin should be pure white with no blemishes, and white finnage should appear delicate with smooth, well formed edges. Pattern, when present, must demonstrate balance and well defined clear edges.

Finally, Karasugoi should not be confused with Shiro-Utsuri or Shiro Bekko, other black and white varieties; in fact the position and ratios of black and white skin are quite different. When a distinct black and white pattern is present on the body of a Karasugoi, it is most usually arranged laterally, from head to tail. Shiro Utsuri patterns tend to be arranged from side to side, over the back, wrapping deeply around the koi; and Shiro Bekko generally have more rounded sumi markings, more common above the lateral line than below it.

Single-Coloured Koi

There is a surprisingly large number of single-coloured, non-metallic koi, some of which have the added feature of a full vignette, fukurin or scale reticulated effect. They may also demonstrate kin-gin-rin scaling, which can be a pleasing enhancement. Included are white, grey, yellow, brown, green, purple and red colours.

The **Matsubagoi** (white, yellow or red basic colours: Shiro, Ki or Hi Matsuba) have a strong vignette, like that of Asagi. A 'pine-cone' effect is given by each scale area, showing a very dark, central wedge.

Of the non-reticulated koi, **Chagoi** (brown) and **Sorogoi** (grey) may also show a light vignette or fukurin effect, formed by the skin covering the extreme outer rim of each scale area, being a darker colour. This lends a very delicate appeal to these koi. The edges of the fins often carry the same fine, dark border, giving the appearance of lace and creating a particularly elegant appearance. Although not as prominent or boldly eye-catching as a true Matsubagoi scaling effect, the definition of the ami, or net, on these koi is an important appreciation point. And when each brown or grey scale area is crisply outlined with black, considerable beauty is added to these otherwise rather plain koi.

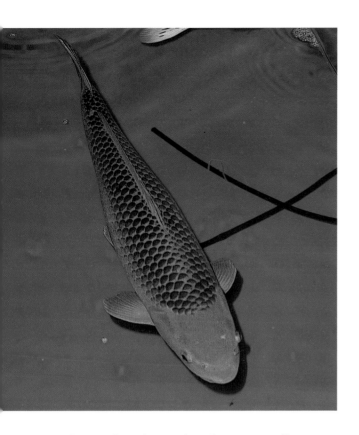

An Aka Matsuba with strong hi and an exceptionally clear vignette.

Another rarely seen Kawarigoi: the Kigoi, this example showing additional kin-rin scaling and the (commonly) red eyes of this variety.

This huge Chagoi has retained a lovely clean finish. The scales show a very faint vignette.

The kin-rin scaling on this lovely Benigoi gives an extra brightness.

Under the bubbles! A once-only seen ki (yellow) matsuba.

Red and White Koi

Red or white koi that are included in the single coloured group are interesting. **Shirogoi** (white) tend not to originate from white fry (Shiromuji) since these are generally culled as worthless, but are koi that started off as something else and 'decolorized'. However, if the quality of the white skin is truly superb, the koi is certainly worth keeping as a rarity.

Akamuji are light red, and are usually culled from Kohaku spawnings, in the same way as Shiromuji. A **Benigoi** is an Akamuji where the hi (red) colour is unusually deep, strong and even. They are rare. If the pectoral fin tips are white they are sometimes called **Aka Hajiro**.

Kigoi

Kigoi are yellow koi and are also descended from Asagi, probably as a natural mutation. Red patches that occasionally appear over the eyes point to the original bloodline features of Asagi. Rarely seen in the UK, a good example should have a bright canary yellow skin with no staining. It has been suggested that the Kijiro, a koi with yellow and white patterns, and even more rare, is a variant of the Kigoi.

Chagoi

Perhaps the most common single-coloured Kawarigoi seen is the Chagoi or brown koi. They are very popular for their phenomenal growth rates, massive final size, and sociable disposition: it is said that introducing a Chagoi to your pond, will help to tame all your koi by their example.

The shade of brown for Chagoi shows tremendous variability, from fawn through to a dark chocolate. From the point of view of appreciation, although the darker brown colours are undeniably richer, the shade is not of prime importance: rather, it is the clarity of the colour and associated fine netting pattern that is vital.

Scaling should look painted on, with high definition; a blurred, 'out-of-focus' finish is very unappealing. No spots (shimi) or stains should be present on the skin. The introduction of kin-gin-rin scaling has added a new dimension to these koi, making them much brighter in appearance.

Chagoi may be described as having a quiet elegance. They are very attractive and loveable koi.

Midorigoi

Midorigoi are true green koi, and tend to be strongly coloured. They are said to be descended from Shusui (doitsu blue koi with a darker blue vignette and laterally arranged red patterns), crossed with

Yamabuki Ogon (bright yellow, single-coloured metallic koi). Traditionally, Midorigoi were always doitsu, but in very recent years, fully scaled versions are beginning to appear. It has been reported that the green colour is not particularly stable over time. A clean head, a strong, clear, true green colour, and neatly arranged scales are the points to look for when appreciating Midorigoi.

Sorogoi

These koi are a delicate grey with a fine, dark vignette or fukurin effect that appears to surround and highlight each scale area with darker colour, as for Chagoi. They are particularly attractive because of this sharp contrast. A fine example of a Sorogoi, with clear, pale grey skin that has no spots or stains is truly impressive. Like Chagoi, high definition of the scale reticulation effect is a vital appreciation point.

Murasakigoi

This purple or lavender-coloured koi is a relative newcomer to the single-coloured group of Kawarigoi. Little is yet known about this variety.

Matsubagoi

These koi are typified by a very strong vignette. Each scale should show a large, wedge-shaped black area, the overall effect giving an impressive 'chequerboard' appearance. Varieties are Shiro (white), Ki (yellow) and Aka (red) Matsuba. Good examples are highly distinctive. Unfortunately they are rarely seen, particularly Shiro and Ki Matsuba. **Aka Matsuba** may develop from Asagi as they age, the hi along the sides of a typical Asagi spreading further and further across the back until no blue colour is left. **Shiro Matsuba** possesses no sumi on the head, a distinguishing feature from Suminagashi. **Suminagashi** also tend to demonstrate a vignette effect, but with the areas of black and white reversed from that of Shiro Matsuba.

The good Matsuba should show a strong and even base colour, a clean head, and most important, sharply contrasting scale reticulation of high definition along the entire length of the koi.

In Summary

This large group of Kawarigoi have one common denominator: a single, although variable colour. It is perhaps worth reiterating that when appreciating such koi, points such as evenness of scaling (kokenami) and quality and uniformity of colour assume great importance, since besides the basic conformation and quality of the koi, there is little else to focus on.

A Sanke-Shusui.

A most unusual crossbred koi, from a Karasugoi / Ogon spawning.

An Utsurimono with true kage. All the white skin is neatly shadowed, while sumi is fully developed.

An unusual non-metallic Kuro Tancho.

Crossbred Koi

Crossbred koi are those that may be said to show some distinct characteristics of both parent lines, for example Sanke-Shusui, Showa-Shusui, Asagi-Bekko, Utsuri-Chagoi. However, because such obviously mixed lineages cannot be directly compared with either parent group (they are too different), they are placed in Kawarigoi as unusual koi. Exceptions in the UK are Koromo-Sanke and Koromo-Showa, classified only with Koromo. Under some show rules (for example, Zen Nippon Airinkai, ZNA) they can be classified with either Koromo or Kawarigoi.

The Problems of Appreciating Crossbred Koi

When appreciating koi like these, difficulties arise. What qualities should be looked for? Which appreciation points of either parent koi should carry most weight? Genetically, the level of expression of particular characteristics might be, and often is, quite different in the crossbred offspring. Considering that it is entirely unpredictable just how much, or how little, each individual koi might resemble either, or both of the original lines, it is impossible to lay down any particular guidelines further than the usual ones governing general appreciation: namely, good conformation (the overall shape and proportion of the head, body and finnage), high quality lustrous skin, a pleasing balance of pattern, and an alert deportment.

With koi such as these, the interest lies in their often very unusual character. They are instantly recognizable as 'different', and trying to find out just what sort of 'Mr Heinz' they are, is a fascinating study. One of the most interesting koi I have ever seen was one with the head of a Karasugoi, clearly patterned in black and white, neatly coupled to a doitsu, lightly metallic bronze Ogon body: strange, but impressive nonetheless since the koi was very large, but it was well proportioned, and demonstrated clear, glowing skin, (see page 93).

Good Examples of Crossbred Koi

Crossbred koi do not appeal to everyone. They can look over-patterned and messy, and often seem to end up with all the worst points of the parent varieties. Nice examples do occur, however, with clean-looking, easily recognizable, well developed patterns, and such koi are very impressive and attractive. The Sanke Shusui (page 93) as an example, is unfortunately a little dark in this photograph, but visible, attractive features from both parent lines include neatly arranged 'Sanke-style' hi patterns along the back, clean white, lightly striped fins (tegima or tezumi) and a deep blue Shusui base. Sumi markings are present, but very difficult to see. This is a koi that clearly shows its origins, yet at the same time represents the 'something strange' of the Kawarigoi group.

This type of koi has been named a Tancho Goshiki. The almost black body looks more like that of a Karasugoi. No Goshiki vignette is visible.

A Gin-Rin Matsukawabake? But the 'black' areas are dark brown! There are also a few light brown patches visible. Is this 'original hi', or colouring from Chagoi lineage?

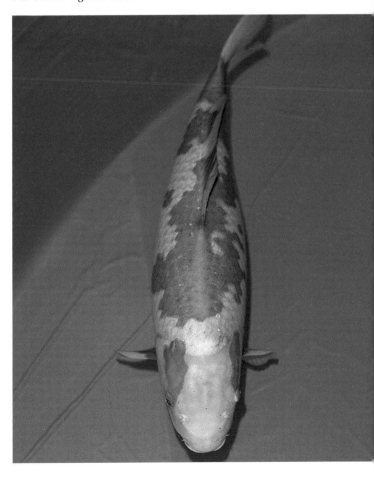

Now very popular, the Ochiba Shigure appears in many shades of brown and grey. A Kohaku-styled pattern is desirable for this variety.

95

A crossbred, or a very unusual Asagi?

An example of a Kanoko Showa.

An elegant Kanoko Sanke.

A menkaburi head is not desirable for Ochiba Shigure.

An attractive doitsu Ochiba Shigure.

The 'Oddities'

This is also a fascinating group. Included are some koi that technically are classifiable with other varieties, but because of their wide departure from the expected norm, cannot with any fairness be compared to them.

Kanoko Scaling

A good example is provided by the phenomenon of kanoko scaling (dappled fawn) seen on Kohaku (white and red), Sanke and Showa (white, red and black but with different pattern characteristics, as described in earlier chapters). The hi does not form distinct, solid markings, but instead is distributed over single scale areas; the appearance is similar to the Matsuba vignette effect, but in red instead of black. The degree of kanoko scaling is variable, and may be mixed with the more usual, solid hi markings. Clearly, koi with kanoko hi cannot be compared readily to those with 'normal' hi alone; hence it is logical to classify such koi as Kawarigoi. If the dappling is strongly marked and evenly distributed, these koi are very appealing. A variation is Gotenzakura, where the kanoko scales are organized into small groups like bunches of grapes.

Kage Koi

Another well known variation grouped with Kawarigoi is that of kage (literally shadowing),occasionally seen on Showa (including Tancho Showa) and Shiro Utsuri, where the white skin has an unusual dark overlay, giving a faint reticulated appearance. Kage also occurs on the red or yellow skin of Hi or Ki Utsuri (other variants of Utsurimono with Shiro Utsuri), and on their metallic equivalents (Hikari Utsuri). Metallic kage koi, however, remain classified with their basic group.

Recently, Kage Showa were reclassified in the UK with Showa, for show purposes, because of the difficulty experienced by benching staff in separating them from Showa with undeveloped (boke) or Tetsu Magoi-line greyish (nabe) sumi. Kage Utsuri remain classified in Kawarigoi. True kage skin in Showa and Utsurimono is in fact quite rare, and good examples even rarer. Ideally the shadowing should be well defined over each individual scale area, though in fact it more often appears blurred or 'out of focus', producing an unappealing, untidy, greyish overall cast to white or coloured skin.

Kuro Tancho

Besides kanoko and kage, koi occasionally appear with a large sumi marking on the head (kuro tancho) and no other sumi on the body. As for kage, metallic koi, which demonstrate a kuro tancho are classified within their metallic group, Hikarimoyo. Very dark (almost completely black) koi with a red tancho marking on the head are a variant of Goshiki. Such koi are also classified with Kawarigoi.

Ochiba Shigure

Finally there is one last interesting member of the Kawarigoi group that could be categorized as either a crossbred or an oddity, but which in fact is gaining popularity so rapidly that it almost represents a new stand-alone variety of koi. The Ochiba Shigure combines the beauty of a patterned koi with the quiet refined elegance of Chagoi. The name means 'autumn leaves on water', and it describes the appearance of these charming koi particularly well. Typically grey and sienna brown, the two colours contrast each other perfectly, and are complemented by a delicate vignette effect in the style of Sorogoi or Chagoi – as always, this should be of high definition and clarity. Patterns are not specified, but are most pleasing to the eye when they are nicely balanced, clear cut, and in sharp contrast with the base colour. The head of the koi should show both colours.

The origins of these koi are not clearly specified. They are most commonly quoted as being natural variants of Chagoi, which in turn originated from Ogon (single-coloured metallic koi) spawnings. Recently, however, reference has been made to Ochiba Shigure being bred from Chagoi crossed with Kohaku, and this would explain the eye-catchingly bright, almost orange-coloured patterns now appearing on some of these koi. Both fully scaled and doitsu Ochiba Shigure occur, and fine examples are now highly prized.

In Conclusion

Appreciating Kawarigoi is perhaps a more personal experience than the appreciation of any other group of nishikigoi: with very unusual koi, what pleases one may be quite unappealing to another. They may have powerful, dramatic impact or understated character and charm. Nevertheless, whilst the well known varieties such as Go-Sanke (Kohaku, Sanke and Showa) appear to be a 'must' for every serious hobbyist, there is definitely a Kawarigoi for every koi lover, to add a little piquancy to quiet summer evenings by the pond.

11 Hikarimuji

Hikarimuji at a Glance

These are single-coloured metallic koi known collectively as Ogon (golden). Colours vary from white to red, with all shades in between. Matsuba Ogon, like the Matsubagoi of Kawarigoi group one, have a reticulated scale effect in a deeper colour, usually black.

Non-Reticulated Ogon

Purachina	(platinum or white)
Cream	(very pale gold)
Yamabuki	(bright gold)
Nezu	(mouse or metallic grey)
Orenji	(metallic orange)
Hi	(metallic red)
Mukashi	(bronze)
Kuro	(metallic black)

Matsuba Ogon (reticulated or vignette pattern)

Gin Matsuba	(silver)
Kin Matsuba	(gold)
Kin Hi	(metallic orange/red)
Mizuho Ogon	(rice ears – a brilliantly coloured doitsu Kin Hi Matsuba)
Kinporai	(a dark bronze-coloured Matsuba)

Not Show Varieties (very early Ogon types)

Kinbo	(black with gold back)
Ginbo	(black with silver back)
Kin Kabuto	(gold 'helmet', black body)
Gin Kabuto	(silver 'helmet', black body)

Not Classified with Hikarimuji for Show Purposes

Kin-Gin-Rin Hikarimuji may be classified as 'B' Kin-Gin-Rin for ZNA shows.

Features

Kin-gin- rin	Rows of very shiny scales along the back and sides.

Doitsu	Either kagamigoi, having rows of large scales along the dorsal and lateral lines only; or kawagoi, having almost no scales at all.
Fukurin	A net pattern, or reticulated effect, fully described in the chapter dealing with kin-gin-rin. Most fully scaled Ogon demonstrate fukurin.

Above: *This cream-coloured Ogon has a slightly darker gold area to each scale, enhancing the attractive net effect, or fukurin.*

Left: *A Purachina or Platinum Ogon, with a lovely clean finish.*

Evolution

The group Hikarimuji is also known collectively as Ogon, literally meaning 'golden'. The first fully golden koi were bred in the 1940s, credited to the work of Sawata Aoki and his family, from a line of originally wild carp found to have golden stripes when captured years earlier. By line-breeding those offspring with the most metallic lustre, eventually black carp with silver and gold heads (gin and kin kabuto) and gold-dusted (sakin) skin were produced. By mating these early metallic varieties with a white koi demonstrating silver markings (shiro fuji), the first fully golden koi resulted. These basic Ogon have since been crossbred with almost every other variety of koi to produce the wide range of always fascinating and often spectacular metallic koi seen today.

Introduction

The single-coloured Hikarimuji comprise one of the three groups of koi that demonstrate a metallic finish to the skin, creating quite a different impression to their non-metallic counterparts. Other metallic varieties are Hikarimoyo ('white-based', with one or more other colour), and Hikari Utsuri ('black-based' in the style of Showa or Utsurimono with one or more other colour) respectively.

Matsuba Ogon

Highly recognizable variants are the Matsuba Ogon group; these show a darker, often highly contrasting wedge of colour within each scale area. A true vignette is created, similar to that seen on Asagi/Shusui (blue, fully scaled and doitsu koi respectively, with a darker blue vignette).

Matsuba Ogon have caused some confusion in the past, since the first impression is of a two-coloured koi; they are thus often misclassified with Hikarimoyo. However, since the colours are merely different shades, with every scale area similarly affected, 'two-tone' Matsuba are correctly classified with the single-coloured Hikarimuji group, rather than as patterned koi.

Matsuba Ogon are coloured white/silver (gin), yellow/gold (kin) orange or red (Kin Hi); all have a black-based vignette. A rare, doitsu Kin Hi Matsuba with brilliant lustre has an individual name: Mizuho (or rice ears) Ogon. Occasionally, dark bronze-coloured Matsuba are seen, called Kinporai.

A magnificent Matsuba Ogon.

Appearance

Hikarimuji may be found in quite a variety of colours from pure white (Platinum Ogon or Purachina), through grey (Mouse or Nezu Ogon), cream, bright chrome yellow (Yamabuki), a light bronze (Mukashi), orange (Orenji) to red (Hi). Most of the colour variations appeared in the late 1950s and early 1960s, and were produced by crossing existing Ogon with other, non-metallic koi, for example Kigoi.

Hikarimuji usually demonstrate a fine netting (amine or fukurin) pattern over their bodies, an important appreciation point for Ogon. The layering effect of skin and scales, the subtle or dramatic difference in pigmentation and lustre between the layers, and the difference in light reflection by scales and surrounding skin, all combine to produce this attractive netting effect. Fukurin is most obvious on the back of the koi, but Ogon with visible fukurin extending to the belly area are said to be highly valued. Hikarimuji may also demonstrate kin-gin-rin (rows of brilliantly shining scales along the back and sides).

This Ogon demonstrates a common conformation problem: the rather short head and a very broad body results in a slightly stumpy appearance.

The slight imperfections of a white nose spot and white-tipped finnage are more obvious on a single-coloured koi like this Kin-Rin Orenji Ogon.

A probably older Kin Matsuba. Note the small pits and discolorations on the head.

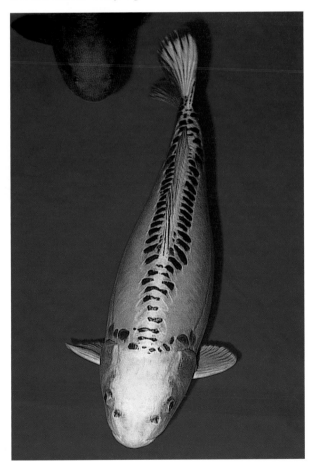

Above: A very neatly finished doitsu Kin Matsuba. Contrast the pectoral fins to those of the Gin Matsuba; these pectorals are small for the size of koi.

Above: Perhaps the most popular Hikarimuji, the Yamabuki Ogon, pure lustrous gold colour.

The scale reticulation on this Kin Hi Matsuba is so precise the effect is almost three dimensional.

Basic Requirements for Appreciating Hikarimuji

Addressing first, as always, the basic requirements of koi appreciation, conformation, (the shape and proportion of the head, body and finnage), and, of course, skin quality, when looking at metallic koi the overall impression is different. The flat reflective finish is far more unforgiving in terms of imperfections, than the soft, non–reflective skin of other varieties. The outlines of metallic koi appear harder, very strongly defined. For example, the rounded trailing edge of the pectoral fin is almost transparent in many non–metallic varieties, especially younger fish, making a deviation from the perfect line hardly noticeable. A metallic koi, however, has solid looking, highly visible finnage right to the very tips. Another point worth remembering, is that since Hikarimuji have no patterns to distract the eye, a good body shape, or lack of it, is particularly obvious. Good conformation then, is critical.

Ogon are thought of as being easy to breed, but high quality, large specimens are difficult to produce since, unfortunately, there appear to be many growth problems fixed in the metallic lines. This might be a

A very lustrous young Gin Matsuba. The vignette is not yet fully developed.

An example of a Kin-Rin Orenji Ogon.

direct result of the early introduction of the European Doitsu carp to the breeding programmes, which has a very different shape from the Japanese fully scaled wild carp. Stumpy, fat Ogon are common, as are those with disproportionately and often misshapen small fins.

Conformation interacts with skin quality for metallic koi in a unique way. The higher the lustre, or reflective finish, the better quality is the skin – but at the same time, the harder is the outline, and the more demanding on basic shape. Superb quality Ogon are incredibly shiny and mirror-like – but such excellence is rarely achieved, especially in the darker colours.

The Head

Looking at individual features, the head of the metallic koi shares with all varieties the important feature of being the first point the eye focuses on. Hikarimuji should have a very clean-looking, 'bald' head with no spots or stains, and a highly reflective finish. Older koi tend to develop darker areas and small pits on the head, which, although lending character and charm, are not desirable features.

Scaling

On single-coloured, rather plain koi such as Hikarimuji, the scales (koke) themselves assume great importance as basic appreciation points. Scaling must be even and symmetrical, particularly on doitsu koi. Rows of scales (kokenami) must be neatly aligned, and lead the eye in a pleasing manner towards the tail. The light netting effect, already described, tends to highlight the neatness of scaling very attractively. Colour on a Hikarimuji should be uniform from nose to tail, although this is difficult to achieve for Orenji and Hi Ogon.

The quality of the vignette on Matsuba Ogon results in a koi showing every single scale area with a discrete, dark wedge that should show no blurring from one scale to the next. Occasionally the rim rather than the centre area of each scale may appear dark, an effect seen more often on varieties including Koromo, Ochiba Shigure and Sorogoi; it is very rare and beautiful on Hikarimuji.

Matsuba Ogon were the variety selected for a series of special prizes at the 1996 All Japan Combined Nishikigoi Show in Tokyo. The group selected for these awards varies from year to year; in 1997 it was Kanoko koi.

In Conclusion

With plain metallic koi it is particularly easy to 'pick holes' and find demerits, but this is not what appreciation is about. It is important to observe each koi as a whole, obtaining an overall impression of what makes that particular koi attractive. Deportment, for Hikarimuji, may play a major role at this point. Much of their beauty derives from their magnificent reflective finnage, which they can display to particular advantage. They also tend to have very charming 'expressions', due perhaps to the slight variability of colour and lustre often appearing on the head around the mouth and nostrils.

Ogon, or Hikarimuji, are undeniably attractive. They have been described as symbols of beauty, in form and hue, with a special fascination all their own. They tend to be widely popular with the general public, and have also been the underlying reason for many hobbyists beginning their collections of koi. Sadly, many koi hobbyists move away from the 'shiny ones' as they discover the other varieties, fostering the idea that Ogon are for the uninitiated only. In fact, appreciation of Hikarimuji has sufficient depth for any level of the art, and it would be wonderful to see a revival of interest in these charming koi, both for their own particular style and for the contrast they provide with other varieties.

12 Hikarimoyo

Hikarimoyo at a Glance

Hikarimoyo may be described as metallic, 'white-based', patterned koi, and they derive from two sources. First, from crossing two differently coloured, already metallic koi – we will call these Group 1; and second, from a cross between a single-coloured metallic koi (Hikarimuji) and a koi from any other non-metallic variety, other than Showa or Utsurimono (see Hikari Utsuri) – this is Group 2.

Hikarimoyo: Group1

Hariwake Ogon	(any combination of two metallic colours, usually a platinum base with gold, metallic orange or red patterns)
Kikusui	(Doitsu Hariwake Ogon originally described with a pattern like that of a Hana Shusui, but latterly all Doitsu Hariwake with orange or red patterns.)
Tancho Ogon	(marking on the head in a colour that does not appear on the body. For example, Kuro Tancho describes a black head marking)
Hyakunenzakura	(rare Kikusui with brilliant platinum dorsal scales)
Hariwake Matsuba	(essentially the same appearance as Kujaku, see text)

Hikarimoyo: Group2

Ginga	(also called 'galaxy', a metallic Matsukawabake)
Platinum Kohaku	(metallic Kohaku, platinum and brilliant metallic red)
Yamatonishiki	(metallic Sanke)
Ginsui or Kinsui	(metallic Shusui, Kinsui has more hi)
Shochikubai	(metallic Ai-Goromo or Sumi Goromo)
Sakura Ogon	(metallic Kanoko Kohaku)
Gin Bekko	(metallic Shiro Bekko)
Tora Ogon	(metallic Ki Bekko)
Kujaku	(metallic Goshiki equivalent. A Hariwake Ogon in appearance with a vignette over both colour components)
Ki Kokuryu	(metallic Kumonryu equivalents)
Kin Ki Kokuryu	(metallic Beni Kumonryu equivalents)

Hikarimoyo

Not Classified with Hikarimoyo for Show Purposes

The ZNA have not finalized a position for Ki Kokuryu (metallic Kumonryu equivalent), although the British Koi Keepers Society (BKKS) has placed it with Hikarimoyo. Under ZNA rules Ki Kokuryu and Kin Ki Kokuryu (metallic Beni Kumonryu equivalent) are currently classified with Kawarigoi.

Kin-Gin-Rin Hikarimoyo may be included with 'B' Kin-Gin-Rin (ZNA shows).

Features

Kin-Gin-Rin	Rows of very shiny scales along the back and sides
Doitsu	Either kagamigoi, having rows of large scales along the dorsal and lateral lines only; or kawagoi, having almost no scales at all.
Fukurin	A net or reticulated pattern. Fukurin is a feature of most fully scaled Ogon.

A common problem for Ogon, a rather 'stumpy' shape. The body and head are not quite long enough for such a solid girth.

Introduction

The show class of the metallic Hikarimoyo provides almost as large a 'catch-all' as Kawarigoi does for non-metallic koi. Hikarimoyo are multi-coloured koi, derived from either crossbreeding differently coloured metallic koi (Group 1); or the metallic offspring of an Ogon (Hikarimuji, single-coloured metallic koi), crossed with another variety other than Utsurimono or Showa (Group 2). Metallic versions of Utsurimono and Showa, characterized by the specific appearance and location of sumi, are classified as Hikari Utsuri.

Evolution

Hikarimoyo are a relatively 'modern' group; for instance, well known varieties such as Kujaku (peacock) only appeared in the 1960s. The majority of non-metallic koi varieties have been crossbred with Ogon to produce their metallic Moyo (more than one colour) equivalents: for example, Yamatonishiki (metallic Sanke), Tora Ogon (metallic Ki Bekko) and Shochikubai (metallic Koromo).

The Basic Principles of Hikarimoyo Appreciation

Some appreciation points for these koi are very specific to the particular sub-group involved and will be evaluated in turn. However, it is vital first of all to remember that the basic conformation (the overall shape and proportion of the head, body and finnage) and skin quality of these koi is, as always, of paramount importance.

Their tremendous range of bright, jewel-like patterns can very easily draw the eye away from defects common to metallic koi – such as a stumpy body, short head and out-of-proportion finnage. Characteristics such as these probably relate to the introduction of the European doitsu carp to the Japanese carp gene pool, in just the same way as for Hikarimuji. Remember! The dramatic, graceful impact of the well proportioned koi should always be looked for first.

Skin Quality

Skin quality is manifest in the shine or lustre, as for the single-coloured metallic Hikarimuji; it is easily visible on the head and pectoral fins, though is sometimes less obvious across the shoulder area because of the patterns on these koi. Good lustre produces an almost mirror-like finish. Ideally no spots or stains should mar the skin or be visible in the finnage. Black stains appearing round the nose

Contrast these two Hariwake Ogons. An appreciation point, very important for doitsu koi,
is a crisp edge to the pattern. Note also the higher impact that the more strongly contrasting colours provide.

Although this Hariwake Ogon has quite extensive
motoaka in the pectorals, by widening the pattern over
the shoulders, a nice balance is achieved with the rather
heavy pattern towards the tail. The hi pattern over the
nose is a charming counterpoint.

This Kujaku shows beautifully clean white pectoral fins.

The quiet elegance of a cream and lemon Hariwake Ogon.

and in the pectoral fins are a common problem for many Hikarimoyo, and unfortunately, the metallic lustre of these koi tends to highlight such defects. Lack of a clean finish can be painfully obvious, perhaps explaining – although it should not excuse – the way many people seem to focus on faults when looking at this group

Pattern

Since we are looking at a group of patterned koi, an additional set of general appreciation points applies:

- A broken or stepped pattern is more interesting than one involving the alternative colour running the entire length of the back (renzokumoyo, or continuous pattern, ippon hi). This also allows appreciation of pattern edges (kiwa). An exception is where the continuous pattern moves laterally as well as from head to tail, a streaming pattern (nagaremoyo), lightening stripe, or inazuma style. The indentations formed by such a pattern do allow some appreciation of kiwa.
- The pattern edges should be sharp, either following the individual scale edges (maruzome, uroko, or scalloped kiwa), or cutting directly across all the scales (kamisori-kiwa or razor border). Interestingly, sashi, usually a valuable appreciation point and detailed in earlier chapters, is not visible on metallic koi because of their reflective finish.
- Colour within the pattern components should give a solid impression, and be uniform along the length of the koi.
- The pattern should be balanced in a pleasing manner side to side (bilaterally) and from head to tail. Unusually, a large white window on the head is a desirable feature for Hikarimoyo, unlike non-metallic patterned koi.

Finnage

The pattern should not run into the finnage. Metallic fins particularly, look best when white and clean, although red fin joints (motoaka) are acceptable if they involve only the maximum of one third of the pectorals. Well balanced motoaka may look very attractive in conjunction with other pattern elements, and can enhance the impressiveness of a specific koi. Unusually for this group, Ki Kokuryu, Kin Ki Kokuryu and Ginga, classified with Hikarimoyo in the UK, typically demonstrate black pectoral fin joints (motoguro)

There is one further exception to the desirability for plain white Hikarimoyo finnage. Light stripes of sumi (tejima or tezumi) in the finnage is a feature of Sanke and Bekko varieties, hence also quite acceptable for their metallic equivalents (Yamatonishiki, Gin Bekko, Tora Ogon).

Group 1 Hikarimoyo: Hariwake Ogon

The two groups of Hikarimoyo may now be examined in detail. Group 1 Hikarimoyo may be thought of as patterned koi deriving from crossing already metallic parents. Offspring are collectiviely known as Hariwake Ogon and have cream. gold, orange or red markings on a silver base. These koi are traditionally fully scaled (Wagoi or Japanese koi), but doitsu varieties (rows of large scales confined to the dorsal and lateral lines only, kagamigoi) have also been introduced by crossbreeding with the European lines. Some of these have no scales at all (leather carp, kawagoi).

Identification and Appearance

The name for Group 1 Hikarimoyo collectively is 'Hariwake Ogon'. Individuals may be further identified by adding the colour and scale pattern to the name: for example, a bright yellow and platinum-patterned doitsu koi may be called a doitsu Yamabuki Hariwake Ogon. Doitsu Hariwake with a wavy pattern of colour confined between the dorsal and lateral scale lines only, in the style of Hana Shusui were traditionally called Kikusui ('chrysanthemum water'). However, in recent years, all doitsu Hariwake Ogon with deep orange or metallic red markings are described as Kikusui, regardless of pattern style.

Traditionally, very sharp contrast between the two colours on a highly lustrous skin was a key element in appreciating Hariwake Ogon. Such koi present a very high impact, especially if the pattern is also well balanced and unusual in its arrangement, with clearly defined edges. Latterly however, the subtle appeal of the much lighter coloured Hariwake has gained notice, for example a platinum base over-layered by a pale yellow or cream pattern. Such koi have an elegance all their own, and it is particularly enhanced if scale lines (koke-nami) are neatly aligned, with fukurin obvious and brightly lustrous.

Hariwake Matsuba

Matsuba Ogon are metallic single-coloured koi that have a vignette where each scale has a darker area either in the centre or around the edge, giving a reticulated effect; they also have a Hariwake equivalent. Theoretically, if a Gin (silver) Matsuba were crossed with a Kin Ki (golden) or Kin Hi (metallic red) Matsuba, then the result could be a Kin Ki or Kin Hi Hariwake Matsuba. However, since Kujaku –broadly,

Above: *Now rarely seen, the metallic Shusui (Gin or Kinsui). The stained head and pectoral fins are common problems for this variety.*

a metallic Goshiki equivalent, Group 2 Hikarimoyo – demonstrate a very similar two-coloured platinum and gold/red pattern with a vignette overlaying both elements, the name 'Hariwake Matsuba' has caused much confusion.

Paler coloured and particularly doitsu Hariwake Ogon with a vignette on only one pattern element, are sometimes still called Hariwake Matsuba, but unless the parents of the koi in question are known, it is difficult to be specific. A distinguishing feature has been said to be the positioning of the dark and light areas of the vignette. For show purposes, since both are classified together, the difference becomes rather academic.

Group 2 Hikarimoyo

Group 2 koi may arise from crossing a Hikarimuji with other non-metallic koi varieties, except Utsurimono or Showa. For example, Platinum Kohaku is the result of breeding Kohaku with a

An interesting metallic 'Goshiki type' in a very traditional style. The metallic grey and strong hi provide an eye-catching contrast, but the head and pectorals are very dark, spoiling the balance of the koi.

Purachina Ogon, producing a silver koi with metallic orange patterns – and this introduces a problem common to all metallic varieties, namely that of faded colours. Thus red tends to be golden or orange, and black is often grey or brownish, depending on the base colour of the koi. Hikarimoyo that have very strong contrasting colours are highly prized, particularly if they are also well proportioned and highly lustrous.

Varieties Rarely Seen

Some Group 2 Hikarimoyo are now rarely seen, for example Gin or Kinsui, the metallic equivalent of Shusui (a blue doitsu koi with a darker blue vignette and laterally arranged red patterns); Gin Bekko (a metallic Shiro Bekko); and Tora Ogon (a metallic yellow or Ki Bekko). Koi like these, although pretty when very young, almost never realize their potential, losing their lustre or colour rapidly as they grow, or developing extensive black areas of skin. Demand for them has consequently diminished.

Another very rare Hikarimoyo is the Shochikubai, or metallic Ai-Goromo or Sumi Goromo, a silver, metallic red-patterned (kin hi) koi with a blue or black vignette effect over the kin hi pattern only. If the kin hi is strongly coloured, in a pleasing, sharp-edged pattern on a clean silver base, and the vignette well defined to each scale area, the impression given by a Shochikubai is powerful indeed, when coupled to excellent basic characteristics of shape, proportion and quality of skin. Occasionally doitsu Shochikubai occur, having the same overlay of blue or black to their basic hi pat-

Only seen once, a fully scaled Shochikubai, a rare koi.

A young doitsu Yamatonishiki. Note the Sanke stripes in the pectorals. Although sumi on the body at this stage is minimal, it is rare indeed to see such a clean finish and strong hi on this variety.

terns. However, because doitsu koi have very few scales, the 'vignette' appears as a less attractive, cloudy finish over scale-less pattern elements.

Yamatonishiki

Yamatonishiki, or metallic Sanke, constitute a better represented sub-group of Hikarimoyo. The doitsu version has recently been described as Heisei Nishiki.

The aim for this variety is a koi having the same quality of hi and black (sumi) markings as the non-metallic Taisho Sanke, coupled with a glistening metallic skin. The appreciation points for Sanke, detailed in an earlier chapter, also apply to Yamatonishiki. In summary:

- The hi pattern is preferably stepped or streamed with breaks to demonstrate clean edges (kiwa).
- The head should show some white skin; a totally red head (menkaburi) gives a very heavy front-ended impression.
- Sumi markings should look solid rather than speckled, and are thought to be more impressive when appearing on the white skin (tsubo sumi) as opposed to overlaying the hi (kasane sumi). Neatly arranged sumi is also desirable.
- Tezumi (or tejima – sumi stripes in the finnage) complements sumi on the body, and is thought to be a sign of sumi pattern stability.

To obtain excellent conformation, beautiful, lustrous metallic skin, as well as strongly coloured, well balanced pattern elements for a Yamatonishiki is a goal much sought, but very rarely achieved.

Kujaku

Perhaps the best-known Hikarimoyo is the Kujaku, the metallic equivalent of the Goshiki, itself a cross-bred koi, usually from Asagi and Sanke lines. Kujaku are reported as being first created by Mr 'Nishi' Hirasawa of Hiranishi Fish Farms in the 1960s, by crossing a Goshiki with a Hikarimuji. A new line, from crossing Matsuba Ogon with Kohaku, has also been mentioned, but not verified by the author at the time of writing.

Like Goshiki, Kujaku have a very complex pattern, and good examples of this variety may compete equitably with Go-Sanke (Kohaku, Sanke and Showa). A basic Hariwake pattern is overlaid with a vignette that is generally expected to extend over the entire koi. However, in more recent years Kujaku are appearing that, like modern Goshiki, demonstrate a vignette largely confined to white skin only: this creates a most interesting and very different impression. Unlike Goshiki in the past, Kujaku have been highly prized for many years, and refined by careful line breeding to produce very clean-looking, high

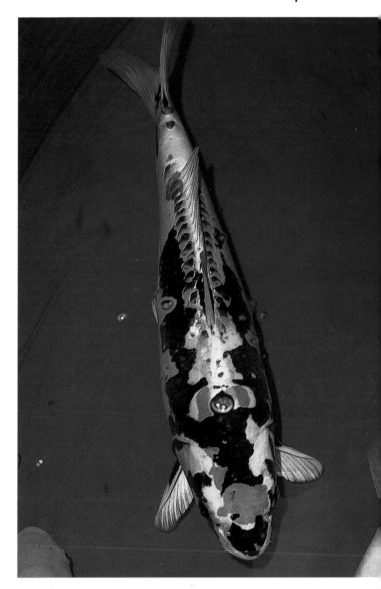

An interesting example of the recently developed Kin Ki Kokuryu.

Although this Kujaku has good lustre and neat scaling, the hi pattern is very heavy, particularly over the head, resulting in a rather gloomy impression.

111

A clean white window on the head is a desirable feature for Kujaku.

A young Ki Kokuryu. The head pattern is neat, but sumi on the body of this koi is rather blurred and light.

An example of a doitsu Kujaku.

One of the rarer Hikarimoyo: A very well finished, lustrous Tancho Kujaku, (or Kin Tancho Gin Matshba).

quality koi. Both fully scaled and doitsu versions are popular with hobbyists.

Both well defined kokenami (scale lines) and Matsuba-style vignette (scale reticulation or netting pattern) are vital appreciation points for Kujaku. In addition, a white window on the head is a desirable feature, and an attractive, sharp-edged, highly contrasting pattern on the body of the koi. As for other metallic varieties, clean white pectoral fins enhance the overall impression.

When the requirements for a top quality Kujaku are added up – namely, excellent shape and proportions, high skin quality (metallic lustre), plus the elements of neat scalation, colour, balance and edge definition of pattern – and then adding quality of vignette as well, their rarity is not surprising.

Ki-Kokuryu, Kin Ki Kokuryu and Ginga

The Ki-Kokuryu is a newcomer, generally classified with Hikarimoyo; it is the metallic equivalent of Kumonryu. The name is a combination of the three characters of the word: 'Ki' or 'kagayaku' means 'light' or 'shining'; 'Koku' is 'black'; and 'ryu' means 'dragon'. Hence Ki-Kokuryu is a shining black dragon. Such koi are doitsu, as are all Kumonryu, and have black and white patterns in the same style.

The lustre on these koi has been reported as being particularly brilliant, but little seems to be yet known about their development and pattern stability. Kin Ki Kokuryu, broadly a metallic equivalent of the Beni Kumonryu, has been reported as being the result of several breeding programmes, for example, from Doitsu Kin Showa crossed with Kumonryu. This means that several styles of Kin Ki Kokuryu. occur, albeit all having metallic red or gold, and silver patterns on a 'black base'. Classifying them can be quite a challenge.

The Ginga or 'Galaxy' is a metallic Matsukawabake, only very recently beginning to be seen at koi shows. At the time of writing, little has been reported concerning this very attractive variety. It appears yet to be too early in the development of all three of these interesting varieties to predict either their final quality achievement, or popularity.

In Conclusion

Hikarimoyo are an interesting, often showy and highly variable group. There is a koi to please all tastes, from the quietly coloured cream Hariwake, to the bold statements made by koi such as Yamatonishiki, Kujaku and the newly emerged Ki-Kokuryu. Although some members of this show variety are now in decline and rarely seen, for example Kin and Ginsui, it seems likely that Hikarimoyo is a metallic group with a secure future.

13 Hikari Utsuri

Hikari Utsuri at a Glance

Traditionally thought of as 'black-based', Hikari Utsuri have the same sumi positioning criteria as Showa and Utsurimono, as this class contains the metallic equivalents of both groups; these are as follows:

- Sumi is usually present on the head, and particularly the nose, of a Hikari Utsuri. Typical patterning is either as a 'v' (or inverted Japanese Kanji symbol) on the forehead with a separate nose sumi, or as a 'lightening stripe' (menware or hachiware) dividing the head.
- Sumi on the body of a Hikari Utsuri tends to wrap around, over the back and reaching below the lateral line, often in highly asymmetrical, jagged-looking patterns. Sumi may also appear in large blocks.
- Sumi on the pectoral fins of a Hikari Utsuri appears as black fin joints (motoguro), rather than as light stripes in the fins. In some cases the entire fin is black.
- Sumi is expected to appear inside the mouth.

Any one or combination of these characteristics may occur.

Metallic Utsurimono

Gin Shiro Utsuri	(black and silver)
Kin Ki Utsuri	(black and gold)
Kin Hi Utsuri	(black and metallic red)

Metallic Showa

Kin Showa	(black, metallic red and silver)
Gin Showa	(metallic red much more golden, minimal amounts visible)

Not Classified with Hikari Utsuri for Show Purposes

Ki Kokuryu, Kin Ki Kokuryu and Ginga: although 'black-based', their lineage is quite different to that of Showa or Utsurimono. All three varieties are classified with Hikarimoyo in the UK and currently, with Kawarigoi under ZNA rules.

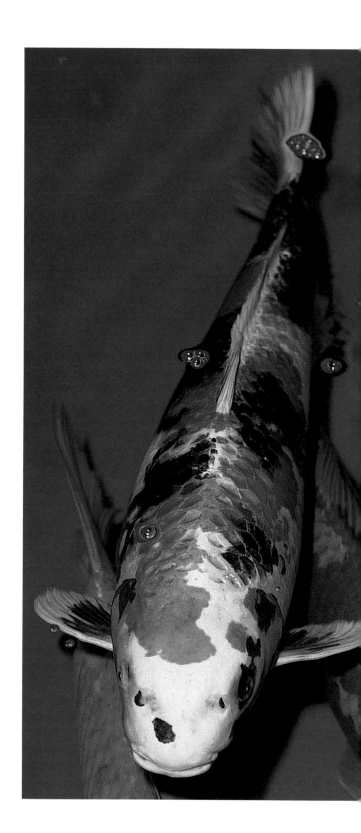

Features

Kage	(shadowed white) may appear on any koi in this group
Motoguro	Black pectoral fin joints.
Menware or Hachiware	Lightening stripe head sumi.
Hanazumi	Sumi on the nose.
Kutchizumi	Sumi on the lips.
Doitsu	Either kagamigoi, having rows of large scales along the dorsal and lateral lines only, or kawagoi having almost no scales at all.

Introduction

At the time of writing Hikari Utsuri are still very difficult to produce, and so are probably the least well represented koi variety at shows; yet these are koi with tremendous presence and beauty, worthy of appreciation at all levels.

Although Hikari Utsuri may be thought of as 'black-based' metallic koi, it is more correct to view them as the metallic offspring of an Ogon crossed with either Utsurimono (non-metallic, two-coloured, 'black-based' with white/red/yellow patterns) or Showa (non-metallic, 'black-based' with red and white). Doitsu (either kagamigoi, having rows of large scales along the dorsal and lateral lines only, or kawagoi, having almost no scales at all) versions of Hikari Utsuri also occur. No Hikari Utsuri 'breed true' with reliable consistency as regards quality, and they must always be produced by the original cross.

Basic Principles of Hikari Utsuri Appreciation

Hikari Utsuri from Utsurimono lines are named by adding 'kin' (gold) or 'gin' (silver) to the original name. Hence a metallic Shiro Utsuri, black and white, would be a Gin Shiro Utsuri, black and silver; and a metallic Hi Utsuri, black and red, becomes a Kin Hi Utsuri, black and a golden orange. Colours are usually lighter in shade on metallic koi than on their non-metallic counterparts.

A metallic Showa is called a Kin Showa.

Above: *Although the sumi lacks neatness at the edges and the metallic lustre is not strong, this unusual Gin-Rin Gin Shiro Utsuri provides an attractive impression.*

Above right: *An attractive and well finished example of a Kin Hi Utsuri.*

A Kin Showa with clear white skin, strong hi and sumi plus a neatly balanced pattern.

Hikari Utsuri

Originally, both Kin and Gin Showa were named according to the proportion of red patterns (hi) on the koi. Gin Showa have less hi. More recently however, all metallic Showa are named Kin Showa.

Conformation

The figure, or conformation (the overall shape and proportion of the head, body and finnage) of Hikari Utsuri is an area to be examined very carefully. On koi with large areas of black skin (sumi), defects of conformation are not always easy to see. As for all koi, a broad, blunt-nosed head should lead smoothly to a wide-shouldered, gradually tapering and well muscled body, particularly demonstrated

by a broad peduncle (the area immediately in front of the tail) in larger koi. A common problem seen in metallic koi is the too short, 'stumpy' body relative to the length of the head. Coupled to this are the poor growth characteristics inherited from the Showa and Utsurimono lines. Koi of these varieties do not readily attain great size; consequently large, well shaped Hikari Utsuri are particularly rare.

Finnage

The proportion of finnage is also a vitally important appreciation point. Metallic koi often have disproportionately small fins, a genetic trait – although in the author's experience this problem is not seen as often for Hikari Utsuri as for other metallic varieties. The shape of the fins must also be carefully examined, ensuring that the leading edge, or ray, is smooth. Well proportioned and displayed finnage adds considerably to the overall impression given. Many koi, particularly of the metallic varieties, really seem to 'show off' in the water, with stunning effect if the finnage is well proportioned and beautifully shaped.

Skin Quality

The quality of the skin for metallic koi is always judged on the level of sheen or lustre; thus very high quality metallic koi have an almost mirror-like finish, incredibly bright. The look of the skin is quite different from that of non-metallic koi, in that there is no depth or softness, and the sheen is flat and reflective.

This does create a problem, in that even quite

Above: *A very unusual Kin Showa. The clear white areas are very eye-catching. However, although the gold borders to the scale areas within the sumi are attractive, unfortunately this probably indicates a lack of depth to the sumi.*

Left: *A truly stunning Gin Shiro Utsuri. It is rare indeed to find such lustrous clarity of finish in this variety.*

Right: *Although technically unbalanced as regards pattern, the pure white face of this Kin Showa results in a particularly attractive koi.*

116

Above left: *The more typical Kin Showa, with rather faded colours.*

Above right: *Rarely seen, a Kin Gin Rin Kin Showa.*

A lustrous Kin Ki Utsuri. This koi demonstrates very heavy sumi, particularly in the finnage, a common problem for this variety.

small imperfections of colour, pattern or scaling are much more obvious. Hikari Utsuri are quite highly patterned, and based on varieties which in themselves present many pattern problems: for example, the break-up of sumi in Hi and Ki Utsuri, leading to much speckling of the red or yellow skin with black. Unfortunately, defects like these appear even more frequently in their metallic equivalents. It becomes clear why so few really top quality, large Hikari Utsuri are seen.

It is perhaps a good moment to stress again however, that koi appreciation should never be about hunting for 'perfection', whatever that is supposed to be, but about what combination of individual features makes a particular koi attractive or outstanding, giving it distinction, character and elegance. Looking at Hikari Utsuri provides a particularly useful example of this very important feature of koi appreciation. Despite their frequent 'bad points', such as scattered sumi, given an acceptable basic conformation and good lustre, they often demonstrate one or more particularly beautiful features which attract the eye: for example, a wonderful, shining white window on a dark koi, or gleaming, bright gold patterning. It is always worthwhile to look for a koi's best points first.

Sumi, Colour and Pattern

Metallic skin is usually brightest if it is white. There is generally an inverse relationship between lustre and depth of colour, with deep black skin appearing quite matt. Highly lustrous Hikari Utsuri tend to

show rather faded colours, an effect exacerbated by the blue background of a show vat. Sumi may appear grey or brownish, red patterns (hi) gold or orange. The metallic colour combinations, although different from the parent Showa or Utsurimono, when bright, have an undeniable beauty. On any metallic koi, the quality of the reflective finish must be given a greater priority than the colour of the pattern elements. It is important to make sure the lustre is obvious on all areas of the koi, including the fins. All metallic koi are also well known for their tendency to blacken, or lose their lustre with age.

Reproducing the same quality and depth of colour as that achievable for the parent Showa and Utsurimono koi is a highly desirable goal, but rarely attained for Hikari Utsuri. There are other points to examine, however. Although sumi may often appear lighter on Hikari Utsuri, it is still important to look for well placed, neatly finished, uniform markings.

Sumi generally appears on the head, and typically, patterns are the same as for Showa and Utsurimono, the 'lightening stripe' (menware or hashiware) dividing the head, or the 'v' on the forehead with nose sumi.

Black fin joints (motoguru) tend to be very prominent in Hikari Utsuri, often to the extent of the entire fin being heavily striped or completely black, which can unbalance the impression the koi presents. Ideally, only up to the inner third of the fin should carry sumi.

The same problem often applies to the body of the Hikari Utsuri, and particularly on those of Utsurimono lineage where very extensive sumi is common, resulting in a rather gloomy finish. The koi with a more 'modern', minimal sumi pattern

Left: *A well finished, lustrous Kin Showa with a kage, reticulated effect over several areas of white skin.*

Things can go very wrong for Kin Showa. Besides a rather small head and pectoral fins, this koi lacks hi. Much of the hi is overlaid by scattered, unfinished sumi. Pattern edges are blurred.

Right: *A dramatic Kin Hi Utsuri.*

of pattern from head to tail. Patterns are viewed as a landscape, leading the eye along the koi.

Ideally all pattern edges should look sharp and well defined. Sashi, the blurring seen on the leading edges of pattern elements of many non-metallic koi, does not appear where there is a reflective finish to the skin.

Some white on the head of a Kin Showa provides lightness, especially if balanced by clean-looking, highly lustrous white pectoral fins and a white area just before the tail. As for metallic Utsurimono, finnage looks best when not too heavily marked with sumi.

It is possible to achieve sumi quality on the head and body of a Kin Showa similar to that of the parent Showa; such quality may therefore be sought, even though it is rarely achieved.

does create a lighter, more pleasing impression for this variety. Delicate silver or gold, or the stronger orange-red looks incredibly lovely, offset by powerful, jagged, but relatively small sumi markings.

As previously mentioned, metallic Utsurimono unfortunately often demonstrate a speckled effect over the white, yellow or orange/red skin. This is caused by the presence of very small sumi spots: these are distracting to the eye, and are undesirable. A clean finish between the two distinct colour elements is far more pleasing.

Metallic Showa include metallic silver/white and gold/orange colours with the sumi. As for Showa, described in an earlier chapter, a pleasing balance between the colours is desirable, as well as a balance

In Conclusion

In summary, the koi of Hikari Utsuri present the koi breeder and keeper with a real challenge. They are difficult to produce, grow on and bring out well, but in the final analysis, added to the undeniable shining beauty of all metallic koi, Hikari Utsuri have an infinite variability of fascinating and dramatic pattern styles, conferring that particular air of distinction and power that koi of the Utsurimono and Showa lines express so well. It would be a real pleasure to see this variety better represented in future.

14 Beyond the First Step

The preceding chapters have aimed to provide a frame of reference, incorporating both general and specific points, of the characteristics that begin a deeper study of koi appreciation. This includes how to go about classifying a koi, how to recognize excellent conformation (the overall shape and proportions of the head, body and finnage), and high quality skin; also what to look for when studying individual varieties and specific koi.

The final area of importance unites the structured approach to appreciation discussed in the previous chapters, bringing us back to our starting point. Perhaps the most vital aspect of appreciation, essentially summing up all other points as well as being the beginning of the road beyond the first step, is the impact each individual koi projects.

Impact

So what are we really saying, when we describe a koi as having 'impact'? Impact in this sense means literally 'forceful influence': to dominate, to impress, to compel attention, even to inspire. It is immediately obvious that such words necessarily introduce an element of subjectivity to koi appreciation, and this is inescapable: to some degree, people will always differ in how they see koi. It is also one reason why a study of the basic aspects of koi appreciation is so important: to bring people closer together in how they look at koi. Learning to recognize individual quality indicators – for example an excellent outline, or solid, deep, lustrous sumi – allows us to better analyse our response to impact.

So we might ask, why does this particular koi create such a powerful impression? It is important to remember at this point that many favourite koi will probably have a great personal impact on us because they possess that element of 'character' which appeals so strongly on a subjective level: they might be very tame, have a charming 'expression', or a very appealing pattern. (This aspect of appreciation is discussed more fully in the introductory chapter.)

Another important response is that of the untrained eye to any koi of massive size. It is bound to look incredibly impressive at first glance, regardless of its quality –

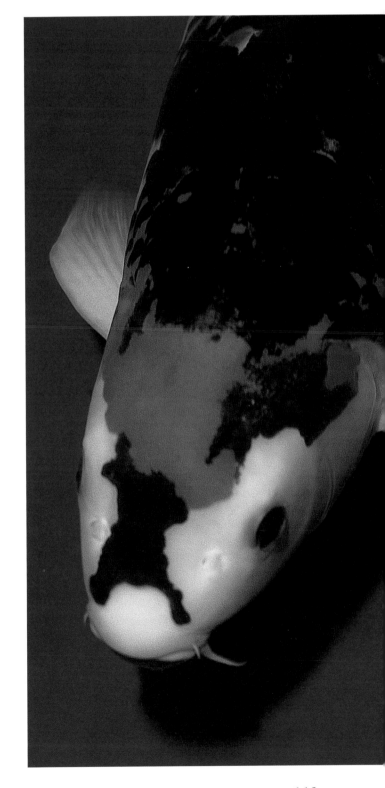

Theory into practice: judging at koi shows.

A pre-show photograph of BKKS judges.

A Kohaku with a particularly memorable pattern.

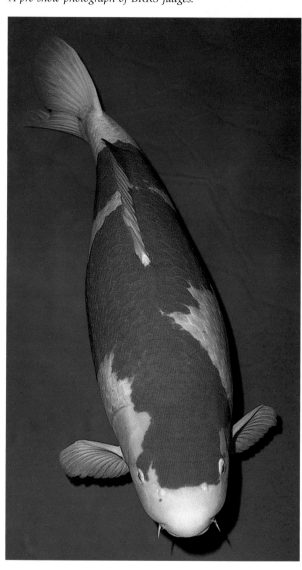

All Japan ZNA 2000 Grand Champion; an over 85cm (33in), high-impact Kohaku of exceptional quality.

Left: *True impact in structured appreciation terms, when everything is working together to create a truly eye-catching impression.*

Right: *A Tancho Showa with incredible impact, created principally by the superb quality of the skin on this koi, which works wonderfully with the fascinating arrangement of sumi.*

Below: *An excellent Kujaku but not especially memorable.*

indeed, an often heard grumble at shows in the past has been that a koi won Grand Champion simply because it was the biggest! Nevertheless, by overlaying the structured, more judgemental approach to our impression, we will be able to assess it more clearly: thus a truly great koi must have incredible impact based firmly on superb quality in terms of conformation and skin characteristics, as explored in preceding chapters.

The Importance of Conformation

For many particularly large award-winning koi, the key to impact is power. For most varieties, a powerful impression is conferred principally by the figure of the koi – but not, it cannot be sufficiently stressed, by size alone. That very special impression of grace and power together depends upon how well the koi is proportioned, and this can only be enhanced when it is accompanied by large size. Add excellence of skin quality, manifest in all its forms for the different varieties, and not easily maintained as a koi grows towards its maximum potential, then well shaped massiveness becomes hard to ignore when appreciating koi!

Above: *What we usually focus on first: the head. Interestingly dramatic patterns catch the eye.*

Learning more about koi; in Southern California.

Below: *The author; a first sight of truly 'jumbo koi' at the 1996 Shinkokai All Japan Show!*

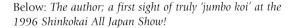

Colour and Pattern

Depth and interaction of colours, and the relative size of pattern elements, also play a vital part in the impression created by a specific koi. For example, Showa do not often gain massive size or bulk and yet they can still produce a very high impact, even when relatively small: the way in which deep, glossy, ebony sumi interacts with solid, bright hi and clear, glowing white skin is almost disturbing in its intensity. Shiro Utsuri also create a very special image, having the same impact on us as might a black and white photograph: the very starkness of the contrast between black and white, particularly with the asymmetric 'jagged lightning' modern patterns, can be quite stunning.

Superseding Basic Appearance

Thus is the first step taken towards a greater understanding of koi appreciation – but it is indeed only the first step, a relatively logical approach that with hard work may be fairly easily learned. But at this point we can no longer look at koi in quite the same way. We must move on. And paradoxically, this means taking a step backwards (metaphorically) in order to see each koi as a whole, rather than focusing on individual elements. The full impact or impression of each koi is often so much more than its shape, its colours or its pattern, studied logically, imply.

The Final Analysis

The way all the elements work together in a unique way for each koi provides a clue as to the essential quality of a truly distinctive champion. It is quite possible to look at a koi and see nothing specifically 'wrong': the shape is good, the skin is clear and bright, the colours strong and even, the pattern neatly balanced with clear edges. Such a koi may easily win its class at a show – but it does not truly attract, it makes no particular impression on you, it is not memorable: in short, there is nothing specifically 'right' about the koi, either.

What is missing is that indefinable message that some koi send so clearly, that element of 'character', a sense of grace, dignity, power, elegance, call it what you will; but it is a feature that sets individual koi apart, and makes them especially eminent. A koi that is impressive in this sense might even be ugly, yet in a charming manner. Every hobbyist will easily recall a koi like this; for example the world famous 'Crown Sanke' and 'Lauren' in Japan, and perhaps the 'Hook Kohaku' and 'Doris' in the UK.

This far more subjective area of the impression that each koi presents is a fascinating study in itself. It is almost impossible to evaluate words such as 'heroicness', 'dignity', 'elegance', or even 'comical' and 'chic' when applying them to the way in which koi impact on us. Yet they are undeniably relevant to koi appreciation. Often it is a key feature on a specific koi which is eye-catching, for example an asymmetric head hi. This is a 'fashion' that has become very popular in recent years, especially for Kohaku and Taisho Sanke, described in detail in earlier chapters. Although every koi with a pattern is essentially 'unique', highly stylized markings often add a special individuality to a koi.

In the final analysis, what we are really seeing when we appreciate koi is a living art form, and its study begins the second step of koi appreciation. The incredible range of impressions given by our koi is breathtaking, and might easily be compared to the huge variability of more conventional artwork. What makes our koi unique, however, is that wonderful extra dimension of their living interaction with us: they are a part of our everyday lives. We should all simply appreciate the harmony, peace and beauty they bring to us: this is truly the magic that is koi.

Glossary

Ago sumi	Sumi on gills
Ai–Goromo	White koi with red markings reticulated in blue
Aka Sanke	Hi covers almost entire head and body
Aka	Basic red
Aka hana	Red nose
Akamuji	Light red koi
Albino	A strain usually demonstrated by red eyes
Ami	Net
Amime	Mesh or 'eyes' of scales in a net pattern
Aizumi	'Blue' sumi i.e. tinged with indigo (high quality)
Aragoke	Large armour scales
Asagi hi	Secondary, undesirable hi appearing as freckles below the lateral line
Asagi Magoi	Forerunner of Asagi, Sanke, Kohaku and Koromo lines
Asagi	Blue, fully scaled koi with its hi usually arranged along the lateral lines and around the cheeks
Atama ga hageru	Clearness of head, clean, clear head
Atama	Head, crown
Ato	Late-appearing (i.e. referring to sumi; ato sumi)
Bekko	White koi with Sanke-style sumi
Beni	Describes deep, solid red
Benigoi	Deep red koi
Beret Hi	Asymmetrical head hi on one side only
Beta gin	Kin-gin-rin where the whole scale shines evenly
Bire	'Fire', a name used for the specific red patterning on Asagi and Shusui
Boke	Undeveloped Showa sumi
Bongiri	The head hi does not come far enough towards the nose
Bozu	No hi on the head, bald head
Bu	Size division
Budo	Arrangement of coloured scales resembling a bunch of grapes
Chagoi	A brown koi
Chigyo	Unsorted fry
Chupa	Medium quality fish
Dagoi	Poor quality fish
Dainichi	Famous Go–Sanke lineage of koi
Danmoyo	Step pattern
Doitsu	German scales, incompletely scaled koi
Doware	Large white area of a pattern
Flowery Kohaku	Many, small areas of hi. No recognizable step pattern
Fuji	The almost metallic finish on the head of some young non-metallic koi
Fukurin	Mesh pattern or reticulated effect (vignette) involving scales and skin
Gaku Hi	Red on upper part of face (forehead)
Giku	Relates to the swimming mode of a koi with a deformed body
Ginsui	Metallic Shusui, may also be called Kinsui
Go bu	Size five
Godan Kohaku	A white koi with a five-step hi pattern
Godan	Five-step pattern
Goma	'Sesame' or scattered sumi
Goshiki	A red and white koi with blue/black scale reticulation on the red and white, or on the white only
Gotenzakura	Cherry pattern
Hachi (atama)	Head
Hachiware	Lightning stripe head pattern
Hachizumi	A black pattern that runs diagonally across the head
Hada	Sheen
Hageru	No blurring on the head (relates to metallic varieties particularly)
Hageshiro	A black koi with white on the head and on the tail and pectoral fin tips
Hajiro	A black koi with white on the tail and pectoral fin tips
Haka Shita	Sagging abdomen
Hanatsuki	Head hi extends down the nose
Hanazumi	A black pattern (or spot) around the mouth and nose area
Hara	Abdominal area
Hariwake	Two-coloured metallic koi from a double metallic cross-breeding
Heisei Period	Contemporary Japanese era
Hi	General term for red
Hiagari	Intensity of the red colour
Hiban	Red pattern element or red area
Higoi	Red koi, usually called Akamuji (light red) or Benigoi (deep red)
Hikarimono	Shining ones, the metallic groups
Hikarimoyo	Multicoloured 'white-based' metallic koi
Hikarimuji	Single-coloured metallic koi, with or without scale reticulation
Himozumi	String-like, thin sumi pattern
Hinomaru	Sun rising
Hirenaga koi	Long-finned or butterfly koi, (not accepted as a koi variety in Japan)
Hiroshima kin-gin-rin	Kin-gin-rin as 'cracked glass' or diamond gin rin. Scales have bright lines running across them.
Hoaka	Hi over the gill plate
Honzumi	'Hard' sumi, indigo black and thought to be stable
Hoshi	Opening or window within the pattern

Ichi bu	Size one
Ichimatsumoyo	Chequered pattern
Inazuma	Lightning-stripe pattern (zigzag)
Ippon hi	Straight hi, renzokumoyo, continuous from head to tail
Iro	Colour
Iroagari	The degree of colour intensity
Iroage	The act of intensifying the various colours
Jari	Gravel
Jarisumi	Small black sumi spots
Jihada	Texture of the koi's skin
Jinbei	Sanke line of koi
Juji	Cross shape
Junidaira Showa	Very old Showa line
Kabuto	Helmet i.e. Kin or Gin Kabuto, the metallic sheen on the head of a black koi
Kagamigoi	Mirror carp, incompletely scaled carp, doitsu or German scaled
Kage	Shadow
Kakutan	Square-shaped tancho marking
Kamisori	Razor border, pattern that cuts across the scale
Kana	Male koi
Kanoko	Dappled hi, appearing on single scales
Kao	'Face'; any area between the cheeks (also known as 'men')
Karasu	Crow
Karasugoi	Crow koi, black koi from the Asagi line
Kasane sumi	Black pattern appearing on the hi
Katamoyo	Single-sided pattern
Kawagoi	Leather carp, few or no scales, classed as doitsu
Kawari	Something strange
Kawarigoi	Strange koi, also known as kawarigoi
Ki	Yellow
Kigoi	A yellow koi, often having red eyes (albino line)
Ki Kokuryu	Metallic Kumonryu
Kikusui	'Chrysanthemum water'; a metallic doitsu Hariwake Ogon with the pattern running between the scale lines
Kindai	Modern
Kin-Gin-Rin	Koi with rows of very shiny scales along the back and sides
Kinitsusei	Uniformity of colour
Kinporai	A bronze metallic Matsuba Ogon
Kinsui	Metallic Shusui with more hi (see Ginsui)
Kinzakura	Golden cherries i.e. gold-bordered hi
Kirekomi	Narrow white inserts into the hi rising from the sides of the koi
Kitchinai	Sanke line of koi
Kiwa	Trailing edge of pattern elements
Kobayashi	Original contemporary Showa line
Koborehi	Scattered red
Koboresumi	Scattered black
Kohaku	White koi with red patterns
Koi	Abbreviated name for 'nishikigoi'; brocaded or jewelled carp
Koke	Scale
Kokenami	Line of scales
Kokesuki	Uneven colour within the pattern i.e. single colourless scales
Komoyo	Small flowery markings
Konjo	Very dark indigo/purple-blue
Konzai	Kiwa having both maruzome and kamisori elements
Koromo	Koi show class including Ai –Goromo, Sumi Goromo, Budo Sanke, Goshiki (non-ZNA), Koromo Sanke and Koromo Showa
Koromozumi	Sumi Goromo netted sumi
Kozumi	Small black spots (but giving a tidy atmosphere)
Kuchi	Lips, a general term
Kuchibeni	Hi on lips
Kujaku	'Peacock'; metallic white-based patterned koi with additional scale reticulation over both pattern and base colours
Kumonryu	Doitsu black koi with white patterns
Kumoru	Loss of colour brightness and gloss
Kuragake	Wearing a saddle': a pattern that crosses the back like a saddle on a horse
Kuro	Black
Kurozumi	Rich, glossy black with no blue highlights
Kutsubera	Shoehorn pattern on the head
Lineages	Genetic lines
Mado	A 'window' in a pattern element involving more than one or two scales
Madoaki	A 'window' in a red pattern
Magoi	Mud carp, originally wild carp
Makiagari	The pattern extending from the abdomen to the upper area
Makikomi	The pattern extends from the upper area to the abdomen
Manzo	Kohaku line of koi
Maruten	Separate head pattern i.e. Marutan Kohaku
Maruzome	'Round-dyed', scalloped kiwa. The pattern follows the scale edges
Matsuba	Single-coloured koi (metallic or non-metallic) with scale reticulation
Matsukawabake	A black and white koi where the pattern transposes over time i.e. summer and winter, although periods may be longer
Matsunosuke	A line of koi famous particularly for Sanke
Men	'Face'; also see kao
Menkaburi	Red covering the entire face/head
Menware	Lightning-stripe pattern across the head (see Hachiware)
Midorigoi	A green doitsu koi
Mizu	Water
Motoaka	Red pectoral fin joints, 'basic red'
Motoguro	Black fin joints
Moyo no kire	Sharpness of edge of the colour pattern
Moyo	More than one (colour)

Mudagoke	Redundant scale i.e. one out of line on a doitsu koi
Muji	Single colour
Mura	A state in which colour is lacking uniformity
Murasakigoi	A purple-/lavender-coloured koi
Nabe sumi	'Soft' grey/brown sumi from the original Tetsu Magoi line; sensitive to light and water temperature; considered unstable
Nagaremoyo	Streaming hi pattern
Namikin	Tail fin
Namitate	Dorsal fin
Narumi Asagi	Colour of traditionally blue-dyed cotton cloth
Nesai	Over one year, and up to two years old
Nezu	Grey
Ni bu	Size two
Niban	Secondary
Niban hi	Secondary hi, also called Asagi hi
Nidan hara	Concave abdomen
Nidan	Two-step
Nidan Kohaku	A Kohaku with a two-step hi pattern
Nishikigoi	'Jewelled carp'
Nosezumi	The black pattern overlapping the red pattern
Ochiba Shigure	'Autumn leaves on the water'; a grey koi with a brown pattern
Odome	Last marking before the tail
Ogon	'Golden'; collective name for metallic koi
Oiya	Koi broodstock
Ojime	Gap between the last pattern marking and the tail
Omoyo	Deep-wrapping pattern
Orenji	Orange
Oyugu hoseki	Living jewels
Ozuke	The base of the tail
Ozutsu	Body area behind the dorsal fin, or caudal peduncle
Peduncle	Area just before the tail
Pongoi	Good quality fish
Purachina	Platinum
Renzokumoyo	Continuous pattern
Roku bu	Size six
Sadazo	Sanke line of koi
San bu	Size three
Sandan	Three-step pattern
Sanke	'White-based' koi with red and black patterns
Sansai	Over two, and up to three years old
Sarasa	Pattern of birds, flowers and geometric patterns
Sashi	Blurring of the leading edge of a pattern element, seen on scaled koi
Sashikomi	Scales covering the front edge of the pattern
Sensuke	Kohaku line of koi
Shiki bu	Size seven
Shimi	Very small black speckles or dots, no larger than a single scale
Shintaro	New Go–Sanke line of koi (Matsunosuke based)
Shiro	White
Shirogoi	White koi
Shiroji	The white area
Shiromuji	White koi
Shitsu	Quality or nature of the skin, including white, hi sumi etc.
Shochikubai	Metallic Ai–Goromo
Shusui	Doitsu blue koi with red markings usually around the sides of the body and the head
Sokozumi	Black that is faintly visible
Sorogoi	Grey koi
Sumi Goromo	White koi with red patterns overlaid by black reticulation
Sumi	Black
Suminagashi	A black koi with scale reticulation in white
Taikei	Conformation of the body
Taisho Sanke	'White-based' koi with red and black patterns; often called just 'Sanke'
Taki	Waterfall
Tancho	Koi with a single, usually red, marking on the head only
Tategoi	Koi possessing potential for the future
Tebire	Pectoral fin
Tejima	Sumi stripes in the finnage
Teri (Tsuya)	Gloss or lustre
Tetsu Magoi	Forerunner of Showa, Chagoi and Ogon lines
Tetsu	Iron
Tezumi	Sumi stripes in the finnage
Tobi hi	Very small hi spots
Tomoin	Kohaku line of koi
Tora Ogon	Metallic Ki (yellow) Bekko
Torazo	'Tiger' Sanke line of koi
Tosai	In its first year, up to one year old
Tsubaki Sanke	Aka Sanke with a chain of sumi running the entire length of the koi
Tsubo sumi	Black pattern over white skin
Tsuya	Lustre
Umebachi	Japanese apricot flower-shaped marking (i.e. Tancho spot)
Uroko kiwi	Scalloped kiwa, see maru-zome
Urushizumi	Jet-black, glossy sumi with a hint of blue (also known as tsuyazumi)
Utsurimono	'Reflections' or 'reflecting ones': two-coloured, 'black-based' koi
Uwappi	Thin hi, no sashi
Wabi/Sabi	Appearance of depth to the skin of scaled koi
Wagoi	Scaled koi
Yagozen	Kohaku line of koi
Yamabuki	Bright gold i.e. Yamabuki Ogon
Yamatonishiki	Metallic Sanke
Yogyo	Young fish
Yon bu	Size four
Yondan	Four-step
Yonsai	Four years old
Yoroigoi	A koi with large armour scales all over its body
Yotsushiro	Black koi with white on the tail, pectoral and dorsal fins and on the head
Zubonhaki	Where the latter half of the body (i.e. tail end) is completely red or black

Right: *A superb Gin Shiro Utsuri.*